TRUSTING THE PROCESS

by Stephanie Sorréll

Illustrations by Hanne Jahr

Science of Thought Press Ltd
Bosham House, Bosham, Chichester, West Sussex
PO18 8PJ, Great Britain

Telephone/Fax: 01243 572109
Email: Scienceofthought@mistral.co.uk

First Published 2000

© Copyright: Stephanie Sorréll 2000
© Copyright illustrations: Hanne Jahr 2000

Published by
Science of Thought Press Ltd
Bosham House
Bosham
Chichester
West Sussex PO18 8PJ
England

A catalogue record for this book
is available from the British Library

ISBN 1 903074 04 5

Cover illustration by Hanne Jahr

Printed and bound by RPM Reprographics
Chichester, West Sussex

CONTENTS

INTRODUCTION

Trusting the Process is a selection of writings from my time as editor of the magazine *New Vision* (formerly *Science of Thought Review*) and also drawn from the eleven years I have spent writing for the magazine prior to becoming its editor. It is the hallmark of my life journey and therefore underlies your life journey too. Our ability to trust what, through the rational lens of the world, seems impossible and incomprehensible, crazy and unknown, comes to test us many times in a lifetime. And although we want to trust and dare the void, we flounder from an intrinsic lack of trust and the wisdom that trust itself is a process. In fact, everything is process! An ever unfolding process which like a river may have many twists and turns before it reaches its destination. Through not accepting this incredible process which we can often only fathom in retrospect, we become lost on the journey and struggle against the current so that we lie exhausted on the bank of the Great Journey until the Divine bids us surrender and try again. Like the great rivers of the world which journey hundreds of miles from their source, we often feel alienated from our spiritual source, forgetting that we are part of the great river and that we carry the source within us.

Process itself is so richly expressed in nature which I believe is the deepest expression of God ever manifest in form. Where there is death and decay the seeds of new life await their beginning. In reality there are no deaths or breakdowns, only transitions and breakthroughs. Our failing lies only in our perception and in the words of Henry Thomas Hamblin, founder of *New Vision*: "If we change our thoughts, we change our life," needs to be invited into our life.

Process like trust is non-linear in contrast to our mechanised methods of progress in the material world. It is an oscillation between visibility and non visibility. Sometimes we are struck by the potency of the inner world, and know that all is well, other times we feel bereft of yesterday's certainty and stranded in the unknown. That is how it is. Sometimes the clouds fall away and we are enveloped in light and warmth, sometimes it is overcast and grey. But we know the sun is always there, whatever the weather. Weather is a process of elements made up of atoms condensing, coalescing, moving faster or slower. And we, as a collection of atoms and elements in a constant state of fluctuation with are subject to the same process, our minds our bodies fluctuation levels of energy. In spring, one day, it seems as if the buds are going to open at any time, then a sudden cold spell puts paid to this. Birds that have taken advantage of the warm trend, lose their fledglings as winter seems to take root again. This is life, this is process, and it is within this matrix of non linear being that trust is born.

We don't always know the answers, we don't have to get it right. And as many wise teachers have said, like Henry Thomas Hamblin and White Eagle, there are no such things as mistakes, only learning opportunities. We are here to learn, to experience, yet we are also here to learn to create and co-create, and become more fully ourselves as divine beings. This is not knowledge that can be accessed with the mind, it is wisdom which can only be divined with the heart.

Trusting the Process is principally about the manifestation of the Divine within our life, our being and work. It is also about surrender, patience and standstills which if we fight against them, disempower and disenchant us instead of empowering us. It is also about change and vulnerability and our need to move forward and embrace them, rather than denying them as we have been taught to in our culture. The book has been divided into five central sections, *Trusting the Process*, *Prayer*, *Nature and the Divine*, *Becoming Real* and *Beyond Thought*.

I do believe, as many do, that we are living at a critical time in our spiritual evolution on this planet; where we are being asked to make the choice between values that profit greed based ventures and exploit the planetary resources rather than honour the earth that we have been given custodianship over. It is no longer a question of blame and judgement, it is taking in hand what we can do to commit more fully to our inner values rather than those of the world. It is easy to curse the darkness, but simple also to light a candle.

Spiritual teachers have abounded throughout history who have pointed out the way. But now it is time to be our own teachers, to walk our talk, to take our own steps of initiative rather than allow others to do it for us, or either put them on a pedestal if they get it right or condemn them if they get it wrong. Our need is to take responsibility, to respond to our many ways of being and the many ways of being of others. In short, seeking scapegoats for our frustration needs to be replaced by not only finding solutions to our problems, but living those solutions. The Divine takes many forms, lives in many rooms which we call religions, but we no longer need to keep our doors locked to each other's faiths rather, in the values and wisdom of Henry Thomas Hamblin, we need to find the spiritual thread that binds all humanity together as one. We also need to connect to each other, but also to the rest of the planet, putting aside racial discrimination and politics that divide and listen to each other. Here in the West we have been guilty of extreme arrogance, impinging our values on the world, without listening to each other's truth and story which is as valid as our own.

This is the only way to the Kingdom of Heaven which is a living paradigm of inclusion rather than exclusion. When we can appreciate that the wounds we inflict on each other and nature are the very tools with which we re-wound ourselves then we can truly recreate the garden of Eden and live the reality which we have for too long reduced to Biblical myth.

PART ONE:
TRUSTING THE PROCESS

DIVINE MEDICINE

If we never met with adversity we should never become strong in character. If we did not pass through experience, often of a bitter and unpleasant kind, we should never learn wisdom. Therefore, we can be sure that the coming year will bring us difficulties and trials, whose object will be to 'extend' us and 'train' us, so that we become strong, yet pliable, steadfast, patient, persistent, and above all, wise with Divine Wisdom.

Henry Thomas Hamblin

As we enter a New Year it is natural to feel compelled to improve ourselves, perhaps to increase our level of acceptance, trust and tolerance. We may feel we need to be more forgiving and loving towards ourselves as well as others.

Henry Thomas Hamblin illustrates in his teaching that there are always going to be conflicts and disappointments. That is a fact. Not because we are unlucky, fated or are being punished by God for past wrongs. Rather, because it is often through difficulty and frustration that we learn humility and grow closer to God. It is through encountering the greatest challenges that test us to the full, when we truly extend ourselves and draw on a greater strength than our own. In many ways we view our conflicts, disabilities, our blocks and actions very negatively. Let's face it, who doesn't in some way ? And a lot of this is due to the misplaced idea that we haven't lived up to impossible expectations either on the physical or spiritual level. We hold a rather outdated idea that if we lived our life perfectly we wouldn't have illness and obstacles. Consequently, we become caught up in this frustration-guilt scenario. The fact is we are not here to become perfect. Created in the likeness of God, we are perfect already. We are here to peel away all the layers which separate us from our realisation of perfection and beauty.

Many of us are working with difficulties and obstacles that are largely lifelong or recurring. And it is tempting to believe that if we were free of that difficulty or obstacle, we could function far more efficiently, be more fulfilled or maintain a greater level of awareness. But again, the very things that we think are *against* as are actually *for* us. It is our perception of our life lessons that is wrong, not the lessons themselves. We need to change our thinking and as this expands to embrace a wider vision, we are able to glimpse the wonderful pattern working out from the seeming chaos.

If we can look upon our recurring difficulties and hardships as 'Divine Medicine' we need to take for the health and well being of our soul, we can perhaps begin to see things differently. None of us likes the idea of taking medicine, even though it is to make us better. Although thanks to modern day techniques we no longer have to put up with the horrible taste which all medicine has been renowned for, we still don't like doing it. Since it is no longer the taste we can blame for our aversion to it, it must be the principle itself. Taking medicine reminds us of our human weaknesses, our vulnerability. And because of that it affects our self esteem. We feel we are failing, or not as strong as we would like to be.

Again the only thing wrong is our perception of it. Too often, we make the mistake of thinking that our happiness is dependent upon our material circumstances and that if we had a different marriage partner, another job, more children or more money we would realise that much sought after sense of inner harmony. But if we begin instead, to realise that our frustrated circumstances are an opportunity to grow closer to God and so birth a lasting sense of happiness, rather than a transitory one based on shifting foundations, we can begin to glimpse the perfection of God's plan. And as so many of us have learned through trial and error, accepting and surrendering to circumstances is the formula for change. As if by magic, the obstacles dissolve. We are working with life rather than resisting what is for our greater growth.

As Hamblin in his teaching often stresses that the more we chase after happiness, the more it eludes us. Happiness, like a butterfly, cannot be constrained, if it is, it dies. Happiness is not an object, although our mind may trick us into believing that happiness is attached to something of material significance or a person. Happiness is a living breathing force which like beauty and peace, its ingredients, cannot be confined or grasped at. The paradox is that very often like the oyster's pearl it is manufactured through irritation and discomfort.

I know that if my life had gone the way I wanted it to, I suspect I would have been a very different person from the one I am today. From a very early age I hated my sensitivity and rebelled against the things that made me different. I wanted to fit into the world, hard though it was, rather than be the girl who saw fairies and had psychic experiences. I was a reluctant disciple on the path. But the more I tried to push my life in the direction of the world, the more I felt as though I was sliding down a slippery slope. Illness forced me to abandon two nursing careers and my generally restless bohemian spirit made it hard for me to settle for any length of time. Often, I felt as though there were impenetrable steel walls looming up in front of the places where I wanted to go. Although I loved writing as, apart from being in nature, it was the only time when I experienced a sense of inner peace, I had a love-hate relationship with my work. And looking back I can see that my medicine has been frustration and limitation caused largely by my strong will. Surrendering has been far from easy for me. It is only now when I am nearing 40 that I realise I have been in the very places and circumstances I needed to be in at the time.

Like Ariadne's yarn that Theseus used to find his way out from the labyrinth, I can see that the thread which I have reluctantly traced through my life has been woven from truth. And what I feared and wrestled with in my greatest darkness was not the dreaded minotaur or monster, but Divine Love itself.

The important thing is that my medicine, like that golden thread, has indirectly led me to where I am now and that your own has led you to read these words. Our medicine may be different but its purpose is to make us whole. And that is the miracle.

We need to remember also that we do walk with angels, every day of the year. Regular communion with our angel will enable us to work with our medicine rather than against it.

THE DANCE OF LIFE

So the darkness shall be the light,
and the stillness the dancing.

T. S. Eliot

To watch the white foamed ambassadors of the sea rushing up the beach, or to see the wind wrestling the branches of the trees is to witness the dance of life. Sometimes we are so caught up in our own personal dance that we fail to participate in this wonderful sacrament of thanksgiving. And living under this illusion of separation, we allow our own dance to overshadow the consciousness that we are all part of the same dance. Each of our steps, however small and insignificant they may appear to be, are an integral part of the Cosmic Dance. As individuals we can be likened to a musical note, a chord. In isolation a single chord can be uninspiring and meaningless, yet when other notes are added a miracle happens. The sequence of notes becomes music.

"Dance, dance wherever you may be," the modern hymn invites. "I am the lord of the dance, said he. I will lead you all, wherever you may be. I will lead you all in the dance."

Because we have made the commitment to live, we are also invited to dance. Reflect on the import of this! We are dancing full time for life!

To acknowledge our part in the dance we need to understand the psychology of dance a little. There are as many dances as there are prayers in the world, but like prayer it is the motive and intent behind the dance that is important, not the technique. As some of us gravitate to different ways of praying culturally and spiritually, so we have different likes and dislikes of dance. Some of us enjoy ballet, others ballroom dance, still others jazz, rock and roll and circle dancing. Those of us who

15

have a great need for independence and are trail blazing a new vision may, like Isadora Duncan, choreograph our own dance. But none of us, however much we feel it, ever dances alone. For if we truly dance to the song of our soul, we open ourselves to the cosmic music which is akin to opening to a force greater than ourselves. We open ourselves to the Master Musician who choreographs our dance. We open ourselves to God.

The Cosmic Dance of life which we are all a part, can be likened to a prism comprised of many facets, each individual, but reflecting the whole. Our personal life resembles one of these facets, yet is simultaneously a part of the Greater Cosmic Dance. As facets in the prism, we all have access to the light that shines through the whole. We are all plugged into the same source. And as dancers we can choose to open ourselves consciously to the whole or remain isolated within our individual facet. Yet when we are aware of ourselves as part of a prism, rather than an isolated facet, we experience a heightened sense of awareness, a sense of belonging and completeness. We hear the sound of the Cosmic Dance and see our own music as a chord and step in the greater dance. That is when we experience a sense of heightened purpose, awareness and joy. We no longer dance alone, whether our dance at the time is one of resurrection, celebration or crucifixion.

As I am writing this I am reminded of a lady I know in her 80s who has visited us at Bosham House many times over the years. Often when I meet her she is beaming; "I've just been circle dancing," she chortles, "for a whole weekend. I feel wonderful!"

This lady has enormous energy and enthusiasm for her age and she puts it down to her circle dancing. That was when her life began, she believes.

By this little example, I'm not advocating that we should all get up and circle dance, although perhaps that wouldn't be a bad idea after all, but rather indicating how energising it is when we realise we can dance, and that our dance is important. Not only physically, but inwardly, because that's where the song really begins.

As circle dancing had brought this lady in touch with her inner song, so are there various catalysts we can use to come into contact with our inner song too, and really this amounts to any activity that gives us a sense of joy; whether it be walking in nature, gardening, meditating, jogging, singing or doing the housework! It is when we are in a state of joy that we are open to the Cosmic Dance and truly in touch with God.

Henry Hamblin writes in his Blessedness lectures: *God has prepared for us joys unspeakable, and infinitely delightful enjoyments, and all that makes for harmony, order and peace; yet, the idea that it is wrong for us to enjoy them, effectively keeps them all away.*

And so it is essential that we keep it in mind and heart that we *deserve* to dance and experience joy, or else what we long for will remain unobtainable. We have to literally become like children in our outlook, because children don't stop and question whether they deserve to be happy or dance, they automatically become caught up in dance and laughter.

Before I write a poem, I am aware of it as a song within me; a dance if you like of vision, concept and feeling. And although that song may be a sad one, the joy comes when I have expressed it. It is as if I have allowed something greater to dance through me. I have in modern day language 'channelled' a force greater than myself. And because it is a healing and regenerative force, it is positive and of the Divine. To successfully become inspired or a true channel we need to surrender the 'self', the ego that holds us prisoner. The 'self' isolates, the Divine integrates.

We all have songs that need to be expressed. How long is

it since we last allowed our spirit to sing?

In Amerindian culture if a native was sick and went to a medicine man for healing, the healer would ask; "How long is it since you last danced?"

That question is a potent one and one that we need to ask ourselves too. How long is it since we allowed God to dance through us? And if not now, then when? As our dear circle dancing friend in her 80s demonstrates, it is never too late to learn.

It may be that when we stand one day in front of our Maker, that we will be asked. "Why did you not dance?"

NAKED WITH TRUST

*All blessings may be ours, if we will but trust Him, instead
of relying upon people, or things or circumstances.*
Henry Thomas Hamblin

I don't think we can ever stop learning about trust, for it
forms the basis of our movement through life. If we cannot dare
to trust, we cannot fully live. Instead we hang back in the
wings, never fully participating in the vast banquet of
experience awaiting us. Although we basically crave for
adventure and joy, our lives become devoid of these qualities
because we hold back from fully committing ourselves. Yet, we
cannot help but envy and admire those who have seemingly
thrown caution to the wind and are living out the Great
Adventure. The beauty of it is that within their commitment to
life, there is a wonderful exhilarating sense of freedom. And
always these people seem to have an endless supply of energy,
whatever their age and physical disabilities ! Whilst those of
us who hold back in our struggle to control our lives, often feel
lacking in energy, direction and joy, feel imprisoned — trapped
by our own desire to be free of commitments.

I often receive letters from readers wanting to know
how to increase their sense of trust. And always their words
touch into my own life experience. Sometimes I have found
life invites us to take crash courses on trust and these are
tremendous learning experiences which can 'fuel' us
throughout the rest of our life. What I have found is that when
I have been without any material means of support, that is
when I have felt God the closest—when all my worldly security
has been stripped away. It is also when I have experienced my
greatest sense of freedom. I have literally had nothing in the

world, or of the world to lose.

In a culture, where priorities are placed on saving and investing money in pension funds and other schemes, we often fail to trust that we have *enough*, but we want *more*. We want to hoard and that works directly in conflict with the trusting process. There is nothing so naked and vulnerable as total trust. And within this framework of living we may wonder why, when we are trusting, the opportunity does not come to make a move either to a new lifestyle or home. We may think it is because the time isn't right, whereas in fact it could be because we are not making full use of the opportunity we have. Maybe we have just enough cash to do what we want to do, but nothing left over. That is trust, it is also risk, but trust and risk go together. We forget God knows exactly what we have in our bank account, if we have enough to do what we need to do, why should he give us more until we need it ?

Trust is as multifarious as the branches of a tree, all of them rooted in the Divine. We may not to be able to trust that other people, or even an organisation can cope without us; that we are irreplaceable. And if this is so, perhaps we may need to look at it another way: Our withdrawal may give someone else the opportunity to help in our place, or, even if we question their capability, it provides them with the opportunity to tap into a greater strength. I remember someone once saying to me: "God is extremely economical." And he is, he makes full use of every situation, turning the negative to the good. What may appear to be an apparent disaster or loss, can be a blessing in disguise. We need to trust to see this.

Perhaps we need to give up our need to control a person or situation. Trusting that the situation will find its course or the person involved will find their own way. Because we feel strongly about a situation, it doesn't necessarily mean we know what is right. Sometimes our opinions get in the way of reality and truth ! The need to control, which we all have to a greater or lesser degree, masks a deep underlying fear of finding ourselves out of our depth and even losing our personal power. Sometimes there is greater strength in letting things be and letting go than in struggling to control.

Often it is not God we do not trust, but ourselves. And this is because we fear ridicule, rejection or dislike. Although it might not be possible for us to like each other, we can on a universal level try to love each other. And the most important thing is that we at least like ourselves, because if we can do that we lose our need for other people's approval and acceptance which in itself can cause so much grief and distress.

Where the world places emphasis on personal power, prestige and strength it is hard to look at our vulnerability in a positive way. Yet vulnerability has a strength of its own which moves us to the core of our being. The vulnerability of a young infant, a new-born creature stirs us to tears. In accepting our own vulnerability, we are more able to see that same vulnerability in others who may initially disarm us with their hardness.

Perhaps we need to trust that someone else's belief system is right for them, rather than endeavour to convert them to our own, which so often results in heartache and misunderstanding. Accepting someone else's differences, whether it be the colour of their skin, culture or religion is a major step in tolerance and understanding.

One of the most overlooked and misunderstood aspects of trust is accepting that the answers and guidance we may receive in answer to our prayers is the right one for us. If we place too many expectations on the answer, we remain blind when the guidance comes and then wonder why our prayers are not being answered.

There are two misconceptions about the issue of trust,

one being that we believe we need a lot of courage and also that we lack the courage. Because courage comes from the heart, it is inherent within us all to the extent to which we open our hearts to the great unknown, which is God. Courage is not a quality available to the chosen few, it is available to us all. And having courage doesn't mean being devoid of fear. It means experiencing the fear and doing it anyway. Fear will always be around in some shape or form, it is the facing of it that makes us strong.

One thing I have found from my own experience as you may have found also, is that there is more fear and heartache in holding back and running away, than facing the challenge. By nature, I would consider myself quite a fearful person, the only thing that has changed is that I have learned to trust that a power greater than myself can work through me if I allow it to. I have come to think less in terms of not being able to do or face something, but more in terms of trusting that the strength and courage will be there when I need it. The more I get my personality out of the way, the better! My personality always limits me, if I allow it to.

The other misconception lies within our believing that trust is passive. Trust is active. It isn't just sitting there waiting for things to fall into our lap, and this is where people may feel failed if they wait and wait and nothing happens. We have to meet God halfway. We have to do what we can, participate in the theatre of life and trust that God will come and meet us halfway. We have been given free will so that we can learn to harmonise it with divine will. We may be frightened of making mistakes and our whole life can be limited by that fear. But out of mistakes emerges a tremendous capacity to learn and expand. Mistakes are as much a part of life as trust. It is our own distorted thinking that attaches an aura of negativity to them. Action is all important and if we ask to be guided it will be Right Action.

One of the finest symbols of trust is the tree in winter. In being stripped naked of leaf and fruit, it somehow encompasses a feeling of dignity. There is no poverty in nakedness, rather a richness and beauty that is unique.

God comes close to us in our nakedness, not only that but he clothes us with garments that are eternal.

THE DYNAMICS OF CHANGE

But of course we cannot remain where we are in a state of satisfaction. If we try to do so, then a time comes when everything appears to go wrong and all our methods fail us.
Henry Thomas Hamblin

Whenever there is a pushing towards change there is always a complementary resistance to that change. Notice that I use the word 'complementary' in a positive sense in that resistance is as necessary as the urge to move forward. Resistance holds the boundaries, it keeps us safe and within the known. Paradoxically, it is the resistance that actually initiates the change because just like the urge to move forward, it is active and powerful. Resistance builds up the pressure, it is the drawing back of the bow string that drives the arrow forward. The greater the force of resistance the faster and further the forward propulsion. In nature, during the spring the buds burst, releasing clouds of pollen and, similarly, without the resistance there would be no explosive force that drives out what is within.

So in this light we can see that resistance, the holding back, is as vital to the whole process of change as the urge to move forward. Problems occur when there is separation and division within the process of change because here vision and perspective become myopic instead of far reaching. Yet as demonstrated so well in nature, the pod that encloses the bursting flower are but two aspects of the same process. Living in a world of duality, of dark and light, warmth and cold, male and female we cannot express one quality without bringing up its opposite counterpart. In ordinary everyday life we can witness these divisions occurring on both a personal and worldly level. Parties becomes divided, countries become ravaged by conflict and families become torn apart. On a personal level this manifests in the form of various ongoing conflicts which hone away at self esteem and our relationship with the Divine. Basically the Divine becomes lost in a miasma of factions that are the symptoms of separation and division.

The great test in all of this is not whether we are resisting change or celebrating it, but in our ability to accept *both* resistance *and* change in ourselves and in others. Can we live with our differences and learn to accept them without wanting to separate, condemn and consequently cause an 'us and them' situation? Can we lose our obsession with defining 'right' and 'wrong'?

This isn't easy at all because it means being willing to surrender our pride along with our need to control and change the 'other'. Yet it is only when we can do this that we can hear and listen to the other and ultimately understand the other's viewpoint and so bring about a reconciliation of opposites. Too often in our efforts to convert, change or override the 'other' we cease to hear the 'other'. Both parties are struggling so hard to make themselves heard that nothing gets heard. Since the 'us and them' situation is the single most cause of prejudice whether it be racial, political, religious or intellectual this is clearly an aspect we need to be aware of on an individual level. Recognising this process taking place within us and acknowledging it, not denying it or condemning it and pushing it back down under, is tremendously liberating. Naming conditions within our soul is a major step towards transforming them. Until we do this, too often we project our unnamed condition onto others and blame others for what we do not own in ourselves.

Change brings up all these factors within ourselves. That is why it is so challenging. I realise while writing this that I am not including all those who find change easy and there are many who do, or seem to struggle with it less. And this is not to say that these have any less of a struggle in other areas despite their openness of soul. And it may be that there are those among us who find 'still' periods difficult and long for an inner freedom that keeps them in a continual state of restlessness. I recognise myself here, although there have been arid years in my life where I not only resisted change, but I resented it because it brought up so much fear.

Change is inevitable, although when we feel stuck in a situation we might have our doubts, but then the change is not always visible, the gradual wearing away of desires and dreams that may block us from the Divine can be likened to the stones on the beach that become smoothed by time.

Change for its own sake has little value, just as change that negates the value of the past and the old becomes separation and denial rather than a movement forward. In actuality it is the old that births the new. We are the fruit of our ancestors, not only genetically but by the various struggles, opportunities and gifts we bear. We carry both the burden and wisdom of the generations and in our struggle for wholeness we bring their wounds into the present and free them.

Within our soul's blueprint we carry the imprints of our past. We may struggle with these patterns that keep re-occurring in our life, resenting the conditions, situations and people who bring them back into being. We may run away from them, but like Francis Thompson's *Hound of Heaven* they come running after us with greater and greater force until we turn and face them, recognising that these same patterns that scourge us with thorns, await our redemption. The past is valuable, priceless and travels with us, ever awaiting transformation and integration within our soul.

It is not important that we resist change or embrace change, because the resistance may be necessary for us, the importance lies in our relationship with the Divine. Since we are by the very nature of life called upon continuously to respond to change or lack of change, it is necessary to re-evaluate and examine our thoughts and feelings towards it, whatever form it takes. Do we resist change because we are afraid of loss and risk or because we genuinely feel the change is not right for us? What level are we resisting on? or do we embrace change because we want to run away from our present conditions that are teaching us valuable lessons or because we feel we cannot grow any more in our present state?

It is important to bring in some of the thoughts of Hamblin here who, years ahead of his time, also received criticism from those who resisted the tide of new thought. His whole life was one of risk and adventure and yet his underlying phrase was "Trust the river that knows the way." And there is nothing stagnant or resisting about a river which sweeps along all onto its course, its journey back to the Source.

He also wrote; "We shouldn't become satisfied with a life of faith in which all our difficulties are resolved by turning to God — we cannot stand still". By this he is embracing the whole quality of movement and change together with the risk and challenge that is evoked. Where there is change there is always risk, living dangerously and loss, but the rewards here are great for they strengthen the soul.

In the midst of change and transition I always find the following axiom important: that Truth itself is unchanging and although its outward form may alter, it is essentially formless, like the Great River or Love. It is only when we become attached to the form, the familiar and the known instead of what it *contains* that it becomes difficult.

Let us take the seed thought change and resistance, meditating on them separately over a period of days and see what wisdom is evoked within us towards ourselves and others. If this becomes a struggle, all the better, something valuable is emerging!

CHANGING OUR VISION

On the way to catch my train, I stopped to watch a blind man crossing the busy main road. It was not the fact that he was blind that made me stare, it was the absolute surety with which he crossed the road, his long white stick tapping the ground before him. Within that surety was a naked trust that the cars would stop to let him pass. If this was not a sure example of trust, I don't know what is.

Trust comes into play when we are blinded to the road ahead and although the territory on either side of us is often in fog too, we know that the only way to go is forward. The road often appears hazardous and uncertain until that moment when we begin to step out into the darkness, and that is when the Universe seems to move forward to aid us, like the cars stopping for the blind man. I think my image of trust will always be that blind man crossing the busy road.

Each day abounds with lessons and opportunities to grasp if we open our eyes to see. The dewdrop on the single blade of grass reminds us that God's grace extends to all. While the mighty trees that bend with the storm to avoid having their limbs torn mirror the necessity of surrendering to circumstances rather than fighting them. A complete stranger may utter a truth in passing that sheds light on an insoluble problem or changes our whole way of thinking. Perhaps harder lessons might materialise in the loss of a loved one or something very precious to us, reminding us of the impermanence of the world of matter so that we seek once again to look for the Eternal and the Infinite. Life is for ever instructing us how to live and develop strength of spirit. Some of these lessons can be as poignant and exhilarating as the notes of the skylark, or shattering as the aftermath of a hurricane where we learn to build our foundation on Eternal truths rather than transient worldly ones. The Great Creative force in life, God, is forever pushing and prodding us toward the ways we need to grow. Sometimes enveloping like an all embracing perfume, other times hard and relentless as He extracts that within us that stands in the way of our greater growth. Henry Thomas Hamblin referred to this shaping and pruning process as Divine Adjustment; in that the eternal and beautiful is forever transforming us so that we can shine in our true brilliance as sons and daughters of God. It isn't always a pleasant or easy process and sometimes like a rose bush that is rigidly pruned in order to grow in greater fullness, this may seem heartless and cruel. But how often we have grown up with the saying that we have to be cruel to be kind. It is really just our way of looking at it that determines our perception. If we change our vision just a fraction our perception changes.

When we are caught up in our individual problems all the events that come into our life, affecting us, changing us are taken personally. Because of this, it is hard to see any experiences in a more objective way. We label these experiences as positive and negative. Even experiences that do not directly affect us such as earthquakes, famine and accidents, we perceive subjectively. We judge them as being good or bad which ultimately affects our well being. And yet weeks, months, even years later we may perceive the same event differently, completely differently. We are likely to see that the things that we initially thought were bad and difficult, had a deeper underlying purpose — a good purpose. It is not the incident that has changed, rather our perception of it has.

I am by no means advocating that earthquakes and famine are positive, but rather that our judgement of these things is subjective and based on our personal experience, our cultural beliefs. It may have very little to do with the true reality.

Since we are seekers of truth, it is important that we have clear vision. As insects and animals will be equipped with the vision they need for their survival, we too are given vision to do what we need to do. Yet compared with the dragonfly and other insects our physical vision is very limited indeed. Many of these flying insects have prismatic vision, others have more than one pair of eyes, some having as many as 32 pairs of eyes. Rabbits and other animals will be able to see behind them as well as in front of them. And the owl is capable of turning its head right round. In comparison with this highly developed visual technology our own vision is poor. It seems strange that such an advanced life form as man should have such limited vision. Although in many ways, because of our modern, although not always advanced way of living, we have blocked out instincts that we had in common with other life forms. We no longer need to know whether there are dangerous animals roaming the streets or even test the weather. We have machines that will do all of that instead. We have transferred these instinctual monitors to machines and highly developed computers that do all of that for us. In many ways our senses have expanded beyond the earth even to the satellites which relay back important information on a global level. And yet God gave us the means to embrace a wider vision. He gave us the means to develop our inner vision. And this has been carried on as an integral and vital part of cultural religions throughout the world through meditation. In all spiritual and religious sects are the wise people, the ones with developed inner vision that can guide a nation or a tribe in times of need. But also within each one of us is the capacity and means to develop that same inner vision too.

If we change our thinking, Hamblin urges, we change our life. And the single most vital thing that affects our thoughts is our vision, our way of looking at things. In order to gain a wider and more spiritual vision, we need to do the opposite of everything society has taught us. We need to close our senses to the world. We need to internalise our vision through meditation. But for those who find it difficult to sit still for any length of time, there are other ways of meditating and broadening our vision. And that is opening our senses to something greater than ourselves. How many of us feel inspired by a piece of music, a walk in nature, a poem?

In order to broaden our vision we need to let go of ourselves and all that we have learnt. As the American poet Walt Whitman wrote: *"Re-examine all you have been told ... Dismiss what insults your soul."* Our knowledge of the world is stark and limited until we apply spiritual vision to it. We need to allow the Divine into our vision. We need to allow ourselves to be as receptive as a child. A child's mind is uncluttered with past experiences and assumptions so it can see things clearly, as if for the first time. Imagine the utter freedom in seeing things for the first time without assumptions and preconceptions!

The more we are able to let go of our past knowledge and open our mind, the more rich and enfolding our experience. The greater our receptivity, the greater our learning. To the degree that we are open to receive new insights is the extent that we are enlightened. And that is what enlightenment is; it is literally *letting the light in*. The more we allow light into our lives the more we grow. In nature an opening flower will turn to the sun and move with the sun, opening and allowing its petals to absorb the light. Climbing flowers will turn and grow, but always before they make another spiral of growth they turn back to the sun for guidance. We can apply this very simple strategy to our own lives. If we feel lost in a fog, and we don't know which way to go, we turn our vision to the light, to God, we open ourselves to search within. And then we move forward in trust like the blind man across the road.

ACCEPTANCE AND CHANGE

One of the secrets of truly successful living is acceptance
By acceptance I mean accepting the experiences of life, and
working through them instead of resenting them on the one
hand, or fearing them and trying to avoid them on the other.
Henry Thomas Hamblin

There are few of us who do not have a problem with
acceptance at some point in our lives. Most of us struggle with
it one way or another on a daily basis either with tangible
worldly issues or inner emotional and mental conflicts.
Ironically, if we have a problem with acceptance, we also have
one with change as well, because invariably change and
acceptance are inseparable. Frequently we find ourselves
caught within the horns of a common dilemma: we are unable
to accept the present situation and we want change, or we find
our present situation intolerable and we are afraid, terrified
even, of the change we know we need.

The dilemma is one of attitude based on our
understanding rather than acceptance and change themselves. I
have found this to be so from my own personal experience. I
used to regard the whole concept of acceptance to be a passive
almost cowardly event. People who accepted difficult events
without fighting and struggling against them had given up their
spirit and allowed themselves to become victimised by
circumstances. But I was confusing acceptance with
resignation, and the two are very different indeed. Resignation
and submission can be carried out with an attitude of
resentment or helplessness. There is often little willingness in
resignation. I have since found that acceptance, far from being
passive, is one of the most powerful things we can do.
Acceptance is an act of great courage. Like peace it is an active

and dynamic force.

The reason why change is so difficult for us is that we have not fully *accepted* the situation we want to change. Once we have accepted it, then the forces of change move in, whether it is a change in attitude which will ultimately herald a change in life events. I find a good example is the seed. Before it can grow it has to accept the conditions it is in, whether it is in a pot, window box or out in the wild. Once it accepts its conditions a commitment is made to grow and evolve.

Acceptance, rather than being a superficial or negative event, is tremendously positive and deep. Sometimes we will say we have accepted a situation and then after some further testing may find that this is far from the case at all! This is because like forgiveness and most states of being, acceptance occurs in progressive stages. It requires time to put down roots and above all, we need to keep affirming deep within our state of acceptance.

Most of us are familiar with the quote; "When the pupil is ready the master appears." To me this is tantamount to the whole process of acceptance and change. When our acceptance is deep enough or when we are ready, change will happen.

I mentioned being afraid to change earlier on and yet knowing that we must change because it is our only way forward. Change is the unknown, the unborn, the unlived and in moving into change there is the fear of loss, the loss of the known. Even though this 'known' may be full of sadness, lack of fulfilment and difficulty, many of us find this more preferable to the unknown and untried that change represents.

In this situation it is important to *accept* that we are afraid. If we fight fear, it fights us. And then go a step forward and instead of looking at fear as negative understand that it is a natural part of our growth and development. Facing fear is difficult, but running away from it is harder, bringing greater stress and anxiety. Accepting fear is the *first* positive step to change. I find it helps to say, "Okay fear, I know you are there. We're going to do this together."

With this willingness to accept fear, change will come. The fear will change. It will begin to unveil the gifts that it has. Like an old familiar dragon it will show us its treasure. If we cannot accept fear than we become caught up in this 'fear of fear' scenario and this is both unproductive and pushes us further away from the change we need.

And the situation that we fear is never what we expect it to be. The situation is simply a new environment for our growth and like the soil that surrounds the seed it contains everything we need for our growth and evolution.

One of the most simple, yet powerful prayers that I have ever come across which encapsulates this whole concept is this universal one:

> *"O God give me the serenity to accept*
> *the things I cannot change.*
> *Courage to change the things I can*
> *and wisdom to know the difference."*

By meditating on these words we can see how inseparable change and acceptance are. Slowly, the wisdom to discriminate between what we need to accept and change enters into the silence of the heart.

THE NECESSITY OF STANDSTILLS

All who seek truth crave for the priceless jewels of wisdom. Despite the innumerable books and discourses available on spiritual enlightenment, they all fail to sate the need within. Nothing comes closer to providing the fodder for wisdom than personal experience. Yet when we come up against a standstill in our outer life, we rebel against it. Desperately, we fight to force our way back on to the well worn tracks of a rhythm we have come to understand. An apparent standstill may arise through illness, depression, bereavement or onerous material responsibilities. And, too often, we see it as an obstacle to our self expression, an unwelcome hindrance. This is because we are looking at it with the concrete mind. With the creative mind and on a more constructive level a standstill provides an opportunity to gain the wisdom we yearn for. It literally forces us to stand still and look within.

Perhaps you can remember being at school and gazing wistfully through the window on to the sun dappled fields outside. And the lesson dragged on and on. Hours of freedom outside the school became precious and the holidays were looked forward to with great excitement.

In a way, this school represents the outer world. There is a daily routine; lessons to be learned together with mental and physical exercises. Whatever our work, we all participate in this school, shaping our lives around mundane daily tasks and preparing for examinations.

Every now and then, when the school term ends, there is an opportunity to gain a greater sense of freedom; to assimilate what we have learned. A standstill is reached. If we view it as an opportunity for further growth and to apply what we have learned we automatically surrender to its influence, allowing ourselves to become caught up in a timeless current of spiritual nourishment. There is no need to gaze wistfully out of the classroom window. Instead, we look through the windows of the soul on to its illustrious plains. We touch the heart of wisdom.

Too often, we find it difficult to accept that term has ended and a new cycle begun. We pace the empty playground in frustration, and sit in the deserted classroom, waiting for things to happen. But they don't because experience is ready to happen elsewhere; within our own self.

These standstills are different for everyone. They may come into effect through a great trauma or as part of the soul's cyclical experience. My own first standstill came when I was seventeen and started training to be a nurse. I was assailed by a period of such intense inner darkness that it disrupted my work. Indignantly, I fought against it, but the more I struggled, the more exhausted I became. I felt like a butterfly beating wings against something impenetrable. I had no choice but to see the standstill through to its agonising end. But, just as unexpectedly as it came, it lifted several months later. For a few days afterwards I felt elevated as if, for a while, I walked in the company of shining angels. My first jewel had been found.

When I was eighteen, it happened again. Once more, I fought a losing battle and found myself facing an implacable wall. When the darkness finally passed away, the light came flooding into my being and I sensed a deep and indescribable love toward my fellow man.

The standstill came every year with astonishing regularity. And it is only now, that I am seeing each standstill as an opportunity to find the wisdom I have always longed for. Crystals and jewels are found deep within the dark caverns of the earth. Likewise, the jewels of wisdom are found deep within the soul. Through our standstills we are given the means of dredging these glittering gems up from darkness into the light, for all to share and appreciate.

Every year nature experiences a standstill in the form of winter, and as Her children we are subject to the very same laws. Pauses are necessary to complement periods of growth and fruitfulness. All growth would make the world into a wilderness, just as all sunshine would make it into a desert.

Through accepting standstills in our life we are learning to transmute knowledge into wisdom. Pupil becomes teacher and starts to tread the path of the great masters...

THE STILL POINT

It is rather ironical that I am writing this in the midst of activity. I had wanted some quiet and space to write this, but instead the morning brought the opposite. Our electrician turned up a day early to do some rewiring in the office and the landscape gardeners are outside creating the new Memorial Garden and will be needing refreshment at regular intervals. Aside from that, an important fax is needing to come through, but the telephone wires are temporarily out of use. Yet, sometimes life is like that. I could become irritated that again the space that I had set aside for something that requires uninterrupted concentration feels invaded and build up nodules of resentment which would make writing even more impossible and create a wall between the workers and myself which makes relationship difficult. Alternatively, I can accept this is how it is, do something else, or work within my limitations trusting that the experience will yield fresh material for processing and trusting also that I will meet my deadline.

The ironical thing was that it had been my *intention* to explore the theme of finding stillness in activity rather than finding a quiet place to tap into that stillness through meditation, yogic breathing or visualisation. In a sense, by the nature of my intention, I set myself up for this experience!

For years we have, cross culturally, sought places of quiet and retreat for inner refuelling. But now although there is an even greater necessity for this today, we also need to *actively* realise the peace within, not just at quiet times, but in the midst of all the demands of our daily life. It is *hard* and it *does* take practice — but it is also possible and, furthermore, it works. Until we develop a willingness to work at this, we will always put peace outside us and feed into a common myth that one day we will find peace; if our circumstances change; if the right person comes along; if we move to the right place or settle within a spiritual community. And in a sense this false myth keeps us at a distance from our still centre, from the Divine. It also becomes an excuse for our not being able to realise peace. Multiple excuses for inner disharmony abound and become objectified into our immediate environment. The people around us aren't right, they haven't got the same awareness, the house we live in is too small, too large, too near the road etc. And again this may be true but it makes realising this still point of even greater importance. Realising peace in the midst of frustration and activity may not immediately change environmental and financial problems, but it *will* change our relationship to them. As Hamblin so often emphasised in his teaching that our environment and the situation we find ourselves in mirrors our inner state of rest and unrest. We draw to us the very conditions we need in order to unleash our greatest potential. I have, over the years, come to realise the truth in this. And, anyway, why not realise that peace within if only to evoke this as a primary prerequisite to changing our conditions, or rather, our relationship to them?

We can long for and wait for change until as my mother would say,"the cows come home". But change actually comes when *we change* our relationship to our conditions. In acceptance, by resting in the still point of the problem and realising the peace in it, change happens. It may come about through a process of precipitation like the formation of stalactites or happen spontaneously and unexpectedly, depending on the complexity of the lesson our soul needs to learn.

Back to this myth that peace is only 'out there', rather than within. In this limiting context we betray our own innate divinity again and again. The still point *is* within and the ironical thing is that the greater the activity, the greater the still point. This works on the same principle as the greater the light, the greater the shadow. The deeper the tree's roots go down into the soil, the greater the potential for stability and branches. In a world of duality the polarisation of one thought or emotion always opens the potential for its counterpart. Lucifer, the brightest angel of all, expressed so well in his name (' Lu' meaning light), was closest to God, yet his mistake cost him his light, his enlightenment. So great was his light that his shadow was equal to this. And herein is a warning, ingeniously expressed in the Greek myth of Icarus with his waxed golden wings who flew close to his sun so that his wings melted and he fell. In this is a lesson for all of us, that we need to include our light and shadow. For in acceptance of our shadow lies the humility that protects us from the blinding persuasive brilliance of spiritual arrogance and pride.

The theme of this article actually came together when I was out for one of my early morning runs. I could hear the traffic on the road and the sounds of morning life, but I was struck by the sight of a seagull poised high above me, wings motionless, just resting, just being. Somehow that sight must have communicated to something deep within me because I seemed to drop down into that still point and experience a great peace. This peace has stayed with me, not just because I hold the image, but because I aligned myself with my true centre.

My days can be busy and demanding with the expanding work here and my studying for an MA in Psychosynthesis Psychology which I am hoping will be useful in the work here. The course takes me up to London a number of weekends a year. Additionally, there are the complexities of living and working on the same premises where the boundaries between working life and my personal life can be very fragile, that is why this still point is of even greater importance to me. If I connect with my innermost centre than I can remain unfazed in the midst of activity. Although I can be tired, I am not emotionally exhausted which can happen when we feel our boundaries and space are invaded. The boundary here is this still point and the only way I can describe it is a sense of letting go, flowing with it, being still in the midst of sometimes frenetic activity.

So often I hear the phrase " the world is getting busier" or "time is going so fast, I can't keep up with it." And in a sense this may be true. I do believe that on a mental level, as a race, we are making quantum leaps in communicating information and networking with each other. This is displayed in our massive advances in information technology. And within this context, our view of the world is changing in the same way that a young infant's does when it masters a new skill, in locomotion or language. I also believe that exciting though this can be on one level, this increase in mental consciousness can make us 'close down' in order not to feel overwhelmed by it all. In this way, connecting with this inner still point becomes essential to our sense of protection. It not only helps us to discriminate between what is important and what is distraction, but acts as a sort of buffer between our over taxed senses and the outside world.

The strange thing is that peace rarely happens if we go running after it. It comes when we open to it, because peace is always there underlying all life, all activity. Changing our relationship with peace, acknowledging that it is here all the time rather than out there can have a profound affect on our sense of well being. In realising that we carry the peace that we are searching after through catalysts such as meditation, prayer and seeking beautiful surroundings give us back our power. But maybe it is accepting *responsibility* for that power that is hard, not the attainment of peace!

The electrician has come and gone and I have been in

and out of my office, talking to him. The landscape gardeners are still here and in the meantime two more men have arrived to put in the new trees. All need attending to from time to time as do my own needs. And part of that attending to my needs is recognising that I can be a centre of peace amidst activity. And in this is an active peace, not an inert peace that can be so protected that it becomes stagnant.

It isn't always easy, and I struggle with connecting with my centre of peace as we all do. But as the Dalai Lama and Buddhists refer to their meditation as practice, so is peace a practice. And we are here to practice !

A WAY OF BEING

Ordinarily, our surface mind, during waking hours, is perpetually in a state of activity. This activity prevents the spiritual mind from functioning; and, as it is only with the spiritual mind that we know God, then it is obvious that it is the activity of the surface mind that prevents us from knowing God.

Henry Thomas Hamblin

How many times have we reached a point in our life when we say " What more can I do?" or " I just can't *do* any more!"

If there is one certain component of the age we live in, it is one of heightened activity. Recently, I wrote about *the still point* in the midst of this often frenetic activity and, judging by the positive response I had from many of you, it seems natural to drop down a little further into the stillness itself and encounter this level of being.

Ironically, I was forced to do this recently through a sudden illness which took me to this place. Illness never visits us without some learning opportunity involved. It enters at a point of dis-ease within the inner or outer life. Sadly, and all too often, unless it is serious enough we either carry on our lives of activity, gritting our teeth against the inconvenience or sit it out feeling sorry for ourselves, waiting for 'it' to go away and leave us in peace so that we can continue living our lives in exactly the same way as before. And often that way of living is being on an endless treadmill of activity as we become lulled into the trance of everyday life or as Charles Tart, Professor of Psychology, names this as "the consensus trance: the sleep of everyday life", which he claims can completely pervade our lives to such a degree that the average person has very little knowledge of their inner or spiritual life.

I remember being very struck by this term when I first heard it and it reminded me of a similar expression I had heard one of the tutors express on a college computer course I attended a few years ago. He described how easily we become hypnotised by screens, whether they are television or computer screens and that it was necessary to take frequent breaks to dissolve the 'spell'.

Why is it then that we become caught up in these maintaining cycles of activity that hypnotise and often anaesthetise our edges? I believe the answer lies in this edge; which represents our area of discomfort and learning opportunity. Symbolically, we describe the 'edge' as a point we are unwilling to go beyond. We use it as a metaphor to describe a place of danger, discomfort, even madness. And yet, it is often in avoiding this edge by constant activity which calms our fears, yet drives us to sensory and mental overload that ironically drives us over the much feared 'edge'.

This inner edge can be points of vulnerability; wounding, fear that evoke anxiety, neurosis or anger sometimes known as the shadow side of our nature. I have come to believe and understand that this edge is where the human broken side of us enters into relationship with the divine. God enters through our broken and vulnerable places, not through our strength which too often needs to be broken down for that entry to take place.

My illness came immediately after a period of non stop activity and, returning from a book fair, I collapsed on my bed and couldn't move for four days when I was forced to seek medical help. But in that time, when I drifted in and out of sleep and I felt myself being stripped of all the activity, I felt something deeper entering into me, a sense of being. I can only describe this as being held in the womb of the Divine and knowing that all is well. Because I had been lacking this sense of being for some years, I was ready for it. Reflective space was a quality that I had missed for far too long and had only succeeded in snatching at in the midst of very full days.

In retrospect I can see that my illness was a call to a deeper level of being. And being in essence is a quality that underlies all activity because it is God. It is not that activity is wrong, it is activity for its own sake; activity without being; activity without drawing from the still centre that causes the blockages both in mind and body. After all, we are human beings, not human doings.

The ironical thing is that out of true being comes right action.

To understand our obsession with doing in our present culture, we need to examine why we allow ourselves to be hypnotised to points of complete and utter exhaustion; because here lies the clue to our edge that we need to look at. In my recent illness I have looked at this and seen that it comes from a deep sense of not doing enough; not giving enough. Really this is a form of inverted arrogance, because by this attitude I am saying that my essential being, which is God, is not enough. I believe that this doing whether it is to become more successful, more liked, more acceptable,more respected, more like the so called 'norm' comes from a Collective Edge that our essential being is not good enough. Driven by our frenzied doing, we hurtle on blindly until an act of grace touches our lives and stills us. Grace presents itself in many forms; illness, exhaustion, even bereavement.

Eric Fromm, who many readers may be familiar with, was an outstanding social scientist and practising psychoanalyst. One of the books he wrote was *The Art of Being*. Here he asks the question 'to have or to be?'. He believed that many of us living in a more luxuriant culture where we do not have to worry about where our next meal is coming from, trade our essential being in for 'having'. In order to make us feel more fulfilled, our values become orientated towards having status, a fine vocation, power, profound insights, better arguments etc. In a sense, crutches replace using one's own feet, one's essential being. Whereas if a person's values are orientated towards being where importance is placed on love, reason and productive work, one is not tied to status, success or career which by their nature are transitory. Because value is attached to being rather than having one is less likely to be devastated if they lose their job or have their status undermined.

Like Hamblin, Fromm believed that people gave up their sense of being in preference to having because they have a built in belief that 'being' is of little worth, or won't work for them. Ambition and status are tangible, whereas being are intangible and mystical.

This is not to say that 'having' is bad, neither Hamblin or Fromm believed that we should go without worldly possessions, but that being or entering relationship with our divine nature comes first, not second.

Although Hamblin was a successful business man it did not bring him any sense of inner peace. In fact, he admitted it made him spiritually ill. It was not so much that he had to give up the business life, but he needed to express his sense of being. Through taking a huge leap of faith and trust he became a successful human being rather than a successful human doing. He put the divine first and the rest followed. By trusting which is a sense of being, we evoke an inner law. Unless we prioritise this inner law, being becomes secondary and, consequently, our lives are half lived.

This dichotomy between being and doing does not only apply to those of us who are 'working' on the external level, but for those who, for various reasons are unemployed, elderly or in other circumstances. Every day we make a choice between being and doing; or rather how we are going to prioritise them. If we begin the day with the emphasis on outer activity and doing without first prioritising our level of being through prayer, meditation, visualisation, taking a walk in nature which in a sense is dropping down to a deeper level of ourselves, we quickly become stressed, disheartened, disillusioned and run up against difficulty. In short we have put ourselves out of relationship with the Divine.

Living in an age where on a spiritual level there are workshops and talks on anything from meditation, Feng Shui to analysing your shadow complex, we need to be discerning too. Of course, we need to learn certain skills, come into relationship with like-minded people and consequently feel better about ourselves, but we also need to stand back sometimes and look at how these activities are serving our Greater Self. Are we exchanging essential being for activity? Are we acquiring more to take us away from our edges that will bring us into greater relationship with the Divine? Is there an element of spiritual competition in our needs where we place value on what we have rather than what we are? Are we following our heart or mindsets of shoulds and oughts?

There is a myth that being is a state of inactivity and yet we only have to turn our vision to nature to see how this 'sense of being' underpins all outer expression. " To everything there is a season....." Let yourself step into the season of being and right action cannot but help follow.

THE QUICKENING

What we call the beginning is often the end
And to make an end is to make a beginning.
T.S.Eliot (Four Quartets)

About 16 - 22 weeks into human pregnancy, the mother experiences what is termed as the 'quickening' which is when the human foetus can be felt moving within the womb. This is sometimes described as the 'turning point'. It has long been believed that this is the time when the soul enters into the body of the foetus. Many of the abortion laws originate from this knowledge.

It is my belief that humanity is now experiencing a *quickening* in consciousness on a world-wide scale around the new millinnium. This is happening on both a collective and a personal level. There is a sense of acceleration, of heightening in awareness together with a dire need to make a quantum leap forward onto a new threshold of being.

There can be no doubt that *despite* the plethora of negativity gripping our media a supreme effort is being made by humanity to avert long standing conflicts in the world. Closer to home, we have been able to witness the positive outcome of the peace agreement taking place in Ireland where at one time, not so long ago, this would have seem impossible. Something that concerns us all are the awesome world debts that blight the development of so many third world countries. It is as if the 'collective unconscious' realises that we cannot move forward or make that quantum leap into the next century unless we release all the old debts. Who wants to take debt, conflict and war into the next era? As we move nearer to the light, which at this time we are by the very nature of our souls being compelled to do, we need to travel light.

The ironical thing is that in releasing others from oppression, poverty and fear we release *ourselves*. Ultimately, whatever we do to others, we do to ourselves, because we are *one body*. Although the world is divided up by rivers, seas, mountains and borders, it is a whole. If you tie a tourniquet around your wrist so tightly that blood cannot get through to feed the fingers, the circulation will stop and the fingers deprived of life will turn blue and be in distress. But it isn't just the fingers, the whole body experiences that distress and will do everything it can do to alleviate and dispel the threat. The liver doesn't say; " Well, it's not my problem. I am not going to get involved." It *is* involved. Every organ, every bone, every cell is intimately involved. The body functions as a whole. Similarly, the sun doesn't say,"I don't like that particular garden, or the people who live in that house, so I'm not going to shine there !" Yet, it is this inane sort of thinking which has dominated the world consciousness in the past, and affects us on a personal level the moment we separate ourselves from the one body, from each other. The moment we call someone a foreigner, then we are exiling ourselves from the one body. It is as ridiculous as saying Jesus Christ was a foreigner because he was a Jew, or Buddha because he was an Indian. By our thinking we have already alienated God, by relegating Him/Her to 'up there'. Whether we like it or not, we are all interconnected and directly involved.

Because it is uncomfortable, painful even, to acknowledge the bloodshed, starvation and injustice going on in other countries where we feel powerless to help, we have in the past slipped into denial. Knowing that there are thousands starving in the Sudan or Bangladesh while we our gorging ourselves on cakes and biscuits, would evoke such a feeling of guilt in us that we would very likely develop an eating problem. Yet, in an unconscious way, this is exactly what has been happening. We have a surfeit of eating problems in the Western world; we eat too much, eat the wrong foods or become anorexic. Every book shop and newsagent's shelves groan under the weight of diet changing regimes which are all based on our deep sense of guilt. Very few of us seem able to live for any length of time without feeling guilty about our diet, how much money we spend or how much we enjoy ourselves. We almost have to ask each other's permission to indulge in any of these areas. Yet, deep down how can we have fun or even go forward and celebrate the millennium when so much of the world is in poverty? It's like sending our hands to a party while our feet are left behind trudging endlessly through a wasteland in search of a few crumbs to eat. It would be a real celebration if our hands could bring something back for our feet to enjoy!

Feeling guilty about wealth our diet and ability to enjoy ourselves does not provide any sense of satisfaction, rather we need to understand *why* we feel guilty; *where* the guilt comes from. We carry the collective debt. We have become spiritually impoverished by the material impoverishment of our fellow humanity. Spiritually, we are in debt. Ecologically, we are in debt. Our continued material progression, if it estranges us further from our sense of humanity with the rest of the world, is on a downward spiral. Quite aside from the political and moral implications of genetic engineering how can we concentrate on 'creating new babies' when there are so many babies dying in our world without care and nourishment. How can we feed more, when we haven't enough to feed our own?

These are painful realisations, yet they have to surface to change. And this is all part of the *quickening* that is taking place in the world. World consciousness is growing at a phenomenal rate, equal, if not surpassing that of technology and it is not necessarily a comfortable process.

In order to integrate these painful realisations within our psyche we have resorted to an ingenious set of labels. We have dubbed countries that are poor as 'undeveloped' and in a mostly unconscious way demoted them to an inferior type of humanity. Those of us who are religious or spiritual, may have slipped them under the heading of 'karma'. "It is their karma to go through this. They have chosen to experience this." Within this network of labels we can struggle to come to grips with realisations that would otherwise cripple us. Except, although this may be true in a sense, we have not understood the whole concept of development in the past. We have seen it as a positive independent entity in itself and not part of a whole. I suspect we have misinterpreted the whole idea of karma, and are seeing it a bit one sided; as if those who are starving and materially impoverished are only here to learn and suffer — not to teach. "God is extremely economical" a friend's words return to remind me. Economical, because God knows that the teacher is just as much pupil as the pupil is teacher. As our consciousness is undergoing a *quickening,* our conscience is growing too as is our sense of compassion. The divisions between rich and poor are falling away. Not only that, but we are understanding that the 'poor' can actually enrich us by awakening compassion within us and teaching us dignity and patience, all the qualities so many of us lack in our culture. As teacher is pupil and pupil teacher, the materially poor are spiritually enriched in a way we can only struggle to understand.

As this truth is being realised and a deepening understanding floods the media, then we are able to act in a different way. The truth literally *frees* us; releasing us from the fears that held us back from letting go, forgiving all the old conflicts, people, situations that held us prisoner in the past.

Many will agree with me when I say that over the past

decade there has been a rigorous breaking down of our belief system, a steady dissolution of dreams we held dear and a painful hacking away of old conditions that held us back. Actually, to be honest, this transformation has been *relentless* ! We've wondered just how much pain we have been capable of bearing as a single unit or person!

But this is now changing. There is a sense of having 'come through' something. There is a sense of movement within, a restlessness, if you like. The *quickening* has begun, not just on a world level where the exorcised world soul is re-entering matter, but there is a feeling of something waiting inside us to be born. Something which will guide us in a more focused way into the future. We cannot define it as yet any more than we can plan our future, because it hasn't been born. I can only describe this as a form of consciousness, a sacred consciousness that will somehow lead us to pick up the broken pieces and begin in a whole new way.

Because we stand at the threshold of a new world era as well as an inner spiritual one, it is important that we follow our deepest intuitions from now on. We are the beginning and the end, the death and rebirth and we carry this duality within our make-up. We are also the dream makers and the dream itself. Old rules and conditioning based on fear and resentment no longer apply. The future is too young and fragile to build and in order to make it stronger we have to truly *live* in the present. If there are things we have always wanted or meant to do or say but never got around to realise, let us act now. Let us *live* our truth, instead of keeping it imprisoned in books, lectures and workshops. By *living* it, we *become* it. We cannot take the old ways into the future, but we *can* take the present we are creating now.

PART TWO:
PRAYER

THE EXPERIENCE OF PRAYER

While all prayer is turning to God, or to an Unseen Power greater far than man, there is a vast difference between the prayer of the beginner and that of an advanced soul, and there are many grades in between. The prayer of the former is an earnest appeal for help, either for deliverance from trouble, or for the satisfaction of some ambition. The prayer of the most advanced worker in the divine art is a contemplation of God. As someone has said of the latter, the soul becomes poised like a bird on outstretched wings, contemplating with ineffable joy and bliss the Infinite and Eternal.

Henry Thomas Hamblin

When I was a child prayer came to me. If I had a problem I went straight to God with it. I had prayers for the animals, the trees, the fairies, other children and adults. There was a simplicity then for I believed that as God had heard me the first time, I didn't need to keep repeating my prayers. Also I hadn't learnt how to pray for myself.

As I became older my prayers became more complicated. I prayed for the conditions in my life to change, to become easier. I prayed for the sort of success that would make me feel a more adequate person. The quality of my prayer lessened and the childlike trust had gone. In its place was a wilful determination to have my life move in the direction I wanted it to go. For a long time it seemed impossible to pray any other way. Basically it was *God's* will and my will. I knew that although I should surrender to God's will it was impossible while I lacked the trust to do so.

It was hardly surprising that very few of my prayers met with a solution. Neither was God deaf. He was eternally there in the silence waiting and listening. It was I who had long

55

forgotten to use the sacred language of true prayer.

After a while, sensing that my prayers were falling far short of their mark, I stopped altogether. Primarily, I felt very bitter about God and his seeming inability to help me. Yet, as time went by, I experienced a sense of relief as if a weighty burden had dropped from me. I had given up the pretence of praying. I had literally given up. And that was probably the best move I could have made, because to understand the nature of prayer, I needed to give up the things that stood in the way of prayer — namely myself and the lack of humility which went with that.

Something else began to develop and grow inside me; a sense of waiting and watchfulness. Within this was a receptivity which took me deep into the heart of nature. During my long solitary walks through woods, across hills, by canals, rivers and streams I became increasingly aware of the vast regenerative force of nature, of life. Again and again I witnessed the humbling breaking down and disintegration of the majestic and beautiful and the emerging of new life out of barren emptiness. Nature became my sanctuary, teacher and companion. Here I found God and slowly discovered the true nature of prayer. It was an ancient secret that slowly bloomed in the human soul and released its healing at times when the personality itself was undergoing some sort of crucifixion I would sit listening to the song of the stream or river, or watch the sun shine through torn piece of sky creating diamond necklaces out of drenched leaves. I heard in nature an eternal hymn of thanksgiving.

Slowly, tentatively at first, I began to pray again. Often, before the words had even left my lips, I would break down as tears streamed down my face. I would falter in the midst of such beauty and simplicity around me. I sensed deep down, that there was no need to pray for things; for in the very acceptance of conditions and a reaching out to a greater strength than my own, prayers were already answered.

Often I just sat or walked and that sitting and walking was my prayer which before, in my fervent need to manipulate God and the circumstances of my life, I could scarcely contemplate. My head had been too full of my own needs to hear that hymn of thanksgiving or appreciate nature's ebullient banquet of beauty around me.

I know this personal experience of prayer may be a very different process for others. I also know that prayer is one of the most misunderstood qualities in our world today. Yet from religion to religion, culture to culture, prayer is universal. This is something we can all do together regardless of class, culture, wealth or poverty as demonstrated by the many world-wide prayer networks and more widely known to us all as the *Silent Minute.*

Yet, in the simplicity and repetition of prayer, its supreme importance may be easily overlooked. Let it be said that prayer uttered from the heart (not to be confused with the emotions) can evoke an effect far beyond our comprehension. And we all agree on the power of thought to have positive or negative sway in our lives and circumstances. The essence of true prayer *is* sacred and therefore *more* concentrated than thought because it is suffused with God.

Because prayer is a living, breathing process, it is something we need to evaluate every now and then. If we, for example, feel 'stuck' in our prayer and lose the sacred sense of the words or its power we need to stop and take check. What sort of prayer are we using to evoke what sort of conditions?

Prayer is a vast subject and therefore it may be necessary to move through the four stages of prayer as outlined by Henry Thomas Hamblin and other great mystics before him. Yet, above all, prayer should always retain its sense of simplicity for therein is its power.

These following stages of prayer which I shall discuss, are ones which we all pass through in our learning and growing process. All are necessary for our greater understanding.

Hamblin referred to the first of these stages as *Petitionary* prayer, where we beg and plead with God for a condition to change or heal. This may be applied to personal or family issues or towards a more impersonal global condition.

The second stage is one of *thanksgiving*, where we realise that God has already answered our prayers and that his blessings are all around us.

The third stage is one of *Meditation* where we meditate on God and become changed into what we meditate on.

The final stage is one of *Contemplation*, where we merge with God consciousness and can bring this back into our everyday life.

I want to stress at this point that we should dispense with the labels of 'lesser' and 'better' with reference to the stages. Anyone with an open and simple heart can access *all* these stages. And different conditions may require different types of prayer. Suffice it to say that as we reach a closer relationship to God, the less use we have of petitionary prayer for ourselves.

THE SILENCE

At the Centre all is stillness. It is the source of all order and harmony. Just as a wobbling wheel becomes apparently motionless if it has been correctly centred, so also do we find peace through our whole personality directly we become centred in God. Jesus asked that those for whom we prayed might be in Him and He in them, thus forming a perfect union and oneness. We experience this when we find ourselves filled with God's Inward Peace, and at the same time we feel that we are being carried along on a river of God's Peace.

Henry Thomas Hamblin

Whether we realise it or not, one of the things that effects us most profoundly in life is silence. It does not matter whether we are old or young, Chinese, British or African, silence holds meaning for us all. There are comfortable and uncomfortable silences, although silence is just silence. Sometimes we find silence embarrassing, empty and depressing, in other instances we find it a welcome refuge and crave for the peace silence brings. Silence is powerful and enduring. It doesn't matter how many times we break it, fill it or run away from it, silence remains.

I talk about silence because I believe this to be the greatest catalyst for true prayer and meditation. By this all pervading silence I am not merely referring to an outer silence; because for one reason or other the quiet we are seeking may not be always available to us. Depending solely on outer quietness for prayer and meditation does not create the strength we may need amidst times of outer turmoil. Rather, what we need to develop is an *inner silence,* a stillness which is ever present at the centre of our being. As prayer is an attunement to God, a union with that divine consciousness, all the thoughts, anxieties and feelings that separate us from that union need to drop away. Notice, I have chosen the words 'drop away' rather than 'suppress'; because although it is tempting to block out all the cumbersome baggage of everyday, it is also impossible. In fact most of us know from experience that the more we try to suppress a feeling, thought or emotion, the more insistent it becomes. Instead, just let it be. If there is noise in the street, acknowledge it and let it go. Let it be.

Before I came to live in the relative quiet of Bosham, I have lived in noisy flats with people's voices sounding through every wall. One cottage had walls and floors which shook each time a juggernaut went by, so I know how distracting this can be when trying to pray or meditate. I also know the value and discipline of sitting *with* it and waiting. Also learning to be comfortable with this waiting. To be aware of the breath, as is often stressed in meditation exercises. There is a process which I can only describe as a 'dropping down' into the stillness. It is as if our intention rises us up on the wings of prayer, but then there is the dropping down into this inner well of stillness as if the spirit is kneeling in prayer. In this stillness our prayer is heard, not because we have spoken it, but because we have humbly surrendered ourselves to something greater. We have let go of self, however briefly that may be.

It is in this stillness that God reads and knows our hearts. When we speak, utter our prayer with our lips or in our thoughts, that is when we hear our prayer. The prayer that God hears may be very different from the one we thought we had expressed.

The one that God hears may be something like this: "Please help my friend who is dying of cancer... help her to find the strength she needs."

The prayer that we uttered might be: "Please help my friend who is dying of cancer to become strong and well again.

Please don't let her die because I will miss her so much."

The difference between the two prayers which are in response to the same cause is that the first is a prayer of the heart, the second a prayer of personal will and need.

Inner stillness and silence is important because this is where true prayer takes place. In the heart there is an emptying of self and God prays *through* us. This is why, very often, although we begin with an intended prayer on our lips, we may utter nothing and instead come out with a profound peace. We have literally entered into the consciousness of God and we know all is well, with our friend, with the world. God's will is working out.

Will based prayers invariably leave us with a sense of frustration and a lack of trust so that we feel we have to keep saying our prayers over and over in an effort to be heard.

True prayer is entering into the consciousness of God and this can only be perceived in the stillness and silence within. When our prayer is united with God it is more likely to be something like this: "Please comfort my friend who is dying of cancer, but don't just help her. Help everyone who is dying of cancer, and the friends and relatives. Help them to be strong. And help me to be a channel for Thy work."

In the silence there is no separation either from God or the rest of humanity. There can only be inclusion in true prayer, not exclusion; for as the scriptures repeat over and over again: God loves everyone equally. He has no favourites. Why should He heal one person to the exclusion of someone else? We may often wonder why one person responds well to healing and another doesn't. But then it is not possible to answer this because we cannot know the divine force influencing each person's life any more than we can know the lessons which the soul may have chosen to learn, or, indeed, the relatives and friends. It is enough that we, in the silence, begin to work with

God. We become the prayers and the healers. God can enter into us when we surrender our personal will to His Greater Will.

I would like to end here with the words of Kahil Gibran which are so comforting and lovely when considering the whole meaning of prayer:

"When you pray you rise to meet in the air those who are praying at that very hour, and whom save in prayer you may not meet."

THE EFFECT OF PRAYER

No prayer is ever lost. Every time we turn to God on behalf of another, a blessing is created which goes on multiplying through Eternity.

Henry Thomas Hamblin

How do I know that my prayers are working? is a question that comes to us all. However strong our faith and intent, there is always the testing time when the 'doubting Thomas' within us questions the validity of our prayer. This may follow a period of intensive prayer for either a person or a distressing global condition. Our patient's situation does not seem to be improving, and the global disharmony far from resolving itself. That is where St Paul's words strike a note of empathy within us: "Lord I believe, help thou my unbelief..."

Doubt is not a failing, rather it is an opportunity which allows us to pray for greater faith. " Help thou my unbelief."

But although prayer may not always appear to outwardly heal a condition, it *will* change and strengthen the individuals involved. I am reminded here of a case which was brought to the fore a few years ago when many people in Britain and abroad were working to release the Russian poet and Prisoner of Conscience, Irina Ratushinskaya. She had been sentenced to twelve years in a strict regime prison camp for writing poetry. Dick Rogers, a priest and surgeon organised a united prayer vigil for her. At the time she was seriously ill, suffering from malnutrition and confined to a sub zero punishment cell.

Irina had noted at the time of the united prayer, despite her gruesome ordeal, that a strength and warmth had flowed into her. Indeed, this experience was shared by all those other women confined in the same prison. She *knew* that people were praying for her. And I think an extract from her poetry illustrates this so well:

Believe me, it was often thus
In solitary cells, on winter nights
A sudden sense of joy and warmth
And a resounding note of love
And then, unsleeping, I would know
A huddle by an icy wall
Someone is thinking of me now
Petitioning the Lord for me
My dear ones, thank you all
Who did not falter, who believed in us !
In the most fearful prison hour
We probably would not have passed
Through everything — from start to end.

Our heads held high, unbowed,
Without your valiant hearts
To light our path.

These words I am sure will touch you as they never fail to touch me: "Thank you all ... who did not falter, who *believed* in us. . ."

In fact it is the prayer, the sustained belief that often brings one through the darkest night of the soul. We must *never* undervalue the power of prayer or think that our effort is having no effect. Fortunately, Irina was released soon after this and now, as far as I know, resides in England.

So here we can see an example of prayer being a tangible living force, bypassing language, distance and culture. Drop a stone into the water and ripples will fan outwards. It is the same when fish leap or dolphins come up for air, ripples are created. Drop enough stones in the water and ripples will spread across the whole expanse. Not only that, but currents will be created where the water finds another route, driven by a greater force. When there is united prayer towards a vision, the concentrated force creates waves, big waves. Prayer wrought consistently does bring about change, but because it manifests initially on an inner level, we may not always see the effect of prayer and give up hope. Additionally when it does manifest on an outer level, it may not be in the way we would hope or expect. If we limit the scope of our prayer with human expectations, we will always be disappointed. If we expect the Divine, then we invite the illimitable to transform and bless.

If we are using petitionary prayer, that is when we are specifically making a particular request for ourselves or others, we might lose heart when our prayers don't appear to be answered. Our friend may not be getting better physically, or the Healing Centre we want may not be manifesting when and where we want. The tactic then is to change our prayer, not give up. When we are asking again and again for the same thing it is rather like banging a door of a safe and expecting it to open. Not only is it very unlikely the safe will open, but we are making too much racket to 'hear' the still small voice. But if we alter the way we pray, so that instead of petitioning, we are asking for the best possible good to come to the situation, we are then using the combination lock. By adjustment, effort and trust we will find the right code to open the door. When we become open in our praying rather than rigid, then the door to heaven opens too, releasing all kinds of blessings and opportunities. At the same time we will find that our thinking has changed. We feel stronger inside, not by way of the will, but on a spiritual level. Prayer is opening ourselves to light and love.

If we merely voice our prayer and allow ourselves to become channels, that is when the miracles really come into being. Maybe our friend's physical illness fails to improve, but instead they become so spiritually awakened that they are in touch with joy and a peace that they have never known before. Maybe our longed for Healing Centre doesn't materialise, but instead we realise we are already moving and living in a spiritual centre and by realising how valuable our work is we too experience joy. With the changed thinking and outlook comes the changed life. When a chemical substance changes it attracts and repels different experiences. When our prayers change and our thinking too, our life cannot fail to change.

PRAYING FOR OUR ENEMIES

... It is a great help to prepare ourselves for prayer by sending out our blessings to all men, especially those who have wronged us and ours, all whom we dislike, and all who have aroused any feelings of resentment and animosity. By blessing them and sending out to them thoughts of goodwill and benediction,- by desiring for them, and declaring for them all the blessings which we, ourselves, enjoy, especially knowledge of the Truth, we prepare ourselves for intimate communion with the Most High...

... If our forgiveness is real, and if we bless genuinely those whom we dislike and against whom we feel resentment, then not only are we ours ourselves forgiven, but we find that our love and forgiveness form an 'Open Sesame' to an inner, intimate communion with the Father of all spirits.

Henry Thomas Hamblin

How much easier it is to pray for the victims of any crime than the perpetrators themselves. And, yet the teaching of Christ is clear. We are urged to not only forgive our enemies. but love them too. How can we do this, when it involves us personally and all we want is to see those who have wronged us justly punished? If we desist from 'casting the first stone' then we long for someone else, an authority of some sort to cast it instead.

On our own, it is rarely possible to achieve this lasting state of forgiveness. But when we admit our powerlessness in this and reach out to God for help, then slowly it becomes possible. Remember, it is always the little earthly mind, the personality that judges and condemns. It is that part of us which aspires to a greater understanding and union with God that forgives. Forgiveness comes through understanding. And that understanding only comes through consistently reaching out to God and praying for understanding. Understanding does come. Little by little, this contact with God filters into the earthly mind and we understand that the perpetrators are sick themselves; that they have had wrong done to them; that they need our healing and prayers just as much as those who have been the victims of crime. Given the same environmental circumstances, the same broken tools to work with, would we have behaved any other way ourselves? Rather than become bitter and defensive about this, isn't it better to admit that we cannot know? There is an old American-Indian saying which, no doubt many are familiar with, that echoes the Christ teaching so well, 'Don't judge a man unless you have walked ten miles in his moccasins'.

I belong to a prayer group and one of the countries we pray for is for Tibet, but we also simultaneously pray for China and the people of China even though they have been the cause of so much suffering and alienation in Tibet. And this demonstrates the whole teaching of forgiveness so well. How can we expect Tibet to change and become healed if we do not pray for the perpetrator — the Chinese as well?

This willingness to forgive our enemies and pray for them is of paramount importance. Because this is how peace develops, not just within the world, but within ourselves. And we are the world. Most of us agree that the outer manifestation of war and turmoil is due to internal conflict and dissension. If we are harbouring repetitive and powerful feelings of resentment towards a situation or particular persons, are we not equally guilty of the same wrong as our so called enemies? By our thoughts we are contributing to the general state of the world. If we cannot be at peace with our brother or sister, plural or singular, how can we be at peace with ourselves and the world.

'Change your thoughts and you change the world' was the essence of Henry Thomas Hamblin's teaching. And in order to move forward spiritually we almost need to use these words in the same way as one would invoke a powerful mantra.

Always the starting point is with ourselves. How many internal wars are we fighting and struggling with each day in relationship to other people? If we can become conscious for a little while of how often we judge and condemn a person, a teaching, system or religion we can gain some insight into the wars we have allowed ourselves to become ensnared in. Is firing missiles of resentment, retaliation and aggression any more noble than firing physical weapons? Think about it!

If we want to feel more at peace with ourselves, then we must rid ourselves of our resentments to others though prayer. As Hamblin says: 'The true object of prayer, then, is to clear something out of the way that prevents our access to the Kingdom of the Spirit.' Then, and only then can we draw into union with God. God is all love and to become a part of that love we must clear everything that stands in the way of that union.

On a personal level, and I am speaking from my own experience too, it is usually those that really rub us up the wrong way, who are teaching us something of real value. If you like, they are by the friction of working with them, allowing us to create a pearl of great price. We might be shown that we need to develop a greater tolerance or even to be more assertive.

It isn't easy to look at it this way; but the person who wrongs us might be pointing to an even greater fault in ourselves. How many times do we hear that through a difficult lesson learned in a relationship, someone has achieved a greater sense of inner strength and direction?

To the extent that we condemn someone, is really the extent to which we need to forgive them; not because we are particularly doing them a favour, but rather we are doing ourselves a favour by learning a valuable lesson.

When endeavouring to develop our spiritual muscles it is easy to slide down into self righteousness; thinking we are spiritually stronger than those around us and, although this is part of the process, it also alienates us from God. Simply because we take a judgmental stand rather than a loving one.

It's not easy, is it? And I would be the first to admit it! And yet wishing the best possible good for our enemies is the only way to be at peace with them and ourselves.

This is not to say that we should let those who rub us up the wrong way, or deliberately wrong us and society get away with everything or walk all over us. We have to speak our truth, make our stand and be true to ourselves, but then we need to release them with love. Release them to God who is all love.

Forgiveness and praying for our enemies is by no means an overnight package, like a sizeable 'bullworker' it tests our muscles. But if we keep asking for God's help and not feel we have to do it all on our own, we will make it easier for ourselves. And little by little as we enter more into the consciousness of God we find our thinking has changed — and our circumstances too.

PART THREE:
NATURE AND THE DIVINE

NATURE AND THE DIVINE

When perfection envelopes the soul however, there is effected a wondrous entry into Nature's realm, and the marvels of creation are revealed without thought and without logic. The trees become radiantly alive... The common fruit becomes a miracle of creation so wondrous that one may weep tears of joy even in the act of holding, say, an apple in one's hand ...

Derek Neville

A couple of months ago I gave a talk entitled *Transforming the Pain into Treasure,* which was really about my experiences with nature and the visionary teaching I have received over the years through my contact with Her. Following this I received several requests to write about this as it had proved to be so helpful for many. I hope what I have learned and am sharing here will be helpful to other readers too.

There is an inner truth running and communicating through all life. A truth that is ancient, sacred, healing and deeply transformative. Above all, it is awesome; for this truth knows no barriers of time, social caste or language. It speaks all languages and is unfathomable as the vast reservoir of space as it as deep as infinity Within this truth lies the miracle of birth, death and resurrection. Here too lies the majesty and strength of the eagle that quests the great mountains, yet also the gentle humility of the snowdrop which blooms silently in the frozen earth.

Writing about this truth often moves me to tears, because I tap into the sanctity and wonder of all creation. Here, at this Source, I drink deeply. An inner communion takes place that is both osmotic and healing. Here, I let go of myself and surrender to this great Source of Being. In surrendering myself I become greater, illimitable and a channel for this language to communicate through. While every atom of my being becomes filled with light, I write poetry, or rather 'that' which communicates through me writes poetry. I can take no personal credit for this; for self has gone.

This is inspiration, drawing in, allowing the infinite to fill me. And this is accessible to everyone, and I mean everyone for it is from this Source that we come and to this Source we return. Our only barrier may be simply a lack of receptivity and an inability to listen. And this I will deal with later on in the article.

From a very small child I have come to know this Source, this truth as Nature. At that early age when I was struggling with the rudiments of the English language, I found the language of nature, of this Source wise and gentle, loving and kind. Like so many children, when I was sad or upset, I would pour out my pain to my surroundings. I would seek comfort from a tree 'friend'; drawing strength from the solidity of the bark; experiencing the life force that moved through it. This is where I first experienced the presence of God and felt it to be maternal and nurturing. To me God was the Great Mother of all creation.

As time passed and I grew older the bond I felt with nature strengthened rather than weakened. Buffeted about by the pressures and demands of the outer world, I sought solace, strength and above all wisdom in nature. Spiritual teachers and books could only take me so far. Although they conveyed a percentage of wisdom and knowledge, it was living truth I wanted. And living truth is always, always first hand.

Nature, this living emblem of the Divine's handiwork, contained all the answers that I hungrily sought. I understood that as a part of nature myself I too responded to the same laws of birth, death, resurrection which are all part of the transformative process.

From the rose I learned that in order to be productive in my growth, I had to be regularly pruned of all old growth that was holding me back and sapping my energy. From the water I learned that in order to hold a clear reflection, it needed to be still. Likewise, and in order to gain a clear vision into my being, I needed to become still through meditation and prayer. And also in order to flow freely like the stream or river, I needed to be clear of blockages. From the tree I learned the importance of letting go of the old leaves, old ideas, in order to let the new buds, new life through. There is the ebb and flow of the sea, the homecoming of the swallows and their return. Everything in nature I learned was cyclical; the emergence of new life, the blossoming, the fruiting process, the stripping away, death and decay. These stages do not just apply to the process of the physical body which is really our outer garment, but to the inward soul. It is a constant ongoing process repeating throughout our lives many, many times. I would watch the stark trees in winter, their buds frozen into clenched fists and understand that in their apparent emptiness they held new life, the future. I would see my own emptiness reflected, where I would approach periods in my life when I had to, like the tree in winter, stand firm and trust, even if I didn't believe that spring would come again. My experience in this world of matter has taught me that it is during my periods of greatest emptiness when I have become filled to overflowing, unexpectedly and without logical reason. New life would surge into me and I would feel inwardly full to bursting. I would understand that my greatest moments of bliss and celebration were born of great personal loss and pain.

I see now, as I am a full time student in a learning process, it is my unwillingness to *accept* the stage that I am at in life that causes me greater pain. How wonderful it would be to be in blossom all the time, to always be fruitful and never need pruning! And yet, would it? It would be both exhausting and impossible. Regeneration and assimilation are as vital to creation as night is to day. But, it is human nature to want things to be different, to become dissatisfied with our present stage. And this dissatisfaction may arise through guilt or impatience. We become impatient with ourselves and then we punish ourselves with guilt in feeling that we should be doing more, giving more — when we should be just being! No wonder we feel awful!

So if we feel stuck, we need to rid ourselves of this terrible weight of guilt we carry around with us. We are learning a lesson of acceptance! If we are impatient, then we are learning a lesson in patience. There are some elements within our make-up, however, that nature doesn't reflect. And these are myths or illusions we live under. Guilt is one of them. I am sure a shrub wouldn't feel guilty about not being in blossom all the time! That is because it is wise, and we desperately need to become part of that wisdom.

But patience ... That really is something else ...

How long does it take an acorn to become a mighty oak or a grub to become a dragonfly?

Years.....

And have you ever waited around long enough to watch a spider weave its web? If the wind tears the fine silken threads, it begins all over again What patience! What fortitude!

When there is so much wisdom, divinity and beauty packed into each small piece of countryside, and even wasteland, is it any surprise that many of us are deeply distressed by the way so-called progress in countries world-wide, including our own, is carving up our land and replacing it with tarmac? As we are all well aware of the global problems facing us at the moment there is no need to depress ourselves with the statistics here. Rather we need to concentrate on what we can do to develop a deeper contact with the earth and save ourselves as well as nature.

We can do this by recognising that there are several stages to union with nature. The first is having to rid ourselves of the illusion that we are separate from nature. It is as much within us as outside us. Nature is no more outside us than God. Nature *is* God in constant expression. Nothing, absolutely nothing in the world exemplifies the whole principle of the crucifixion and resurrection as nature. A forest fire will desecrate a whole landscape, yet in a year or so, life burgeons forth again. Nature holds one immutable truth — after the crucifixion and death, always, always the resurrection. We are no more separate from nature or God than a snail is from its home or a spider from its web. If we use the Bible as a symbol of this, taking the story of Adam and Eve as an example, we have the tree of fruits in Eden in the beginning to represent growth and fertility. And then in the New Testament we finally have the death on the wooden cross; the crucifixion which precedes the resurrection. Death is never a conclusion. That is where we fall into blindness. It is a transition and a resurrection which preludes the rebirth.

Secondly, we have to be receptive. Empty even. How many times do we walk unseeing through a landscape full of busy noisy thoughts or chatter? That isn't visiting nature, the forest or woodland, it is simply taking one's internal or external chatter into nature. That is all. No communication has happened. There has been no osmosis. No communication or sacrament. But being receptive is, allowing nature, this sacred language, to communicate through us. It is allowing ourselves to be a clear channel. In this silence of contemplation are found all the answers to our problems. Be receptive, listen. Breathe in. Become inspired, become filled.

The third quality is storage. We need to store what we

have learned. Use it for reflection, inner nourishment and contemplation. If it helps, bring a leaf or a stone home with you, hold it, contemplate it, see what it tells you about life, about yourself. This method of contemplation is what mystics, Buddhists, priests, monks have used throughout the ages.

'If you cannot understand my silence. How can you understand my words?' are the words that I once saw hanging on a friend's wall. What a wealth of truth conveyed in this simple quote!

I can promise you that if you spare time for nature either by walking in it, or if you can't do this, meditating upon it, you will eventually find yourself slowing down and Her wisdom filling you. This is our service to nature, to the Divine and to each other.

The fourth stage is expression and this is really an act of service. It might not he a painting, or a poem. It might be a gift to a friend of an acorn, leaf or flower or even a richness in your soul which will shine through you. Service is partaking of the wonderful sacrament of creation and going out into the world imbued with its ancient message.

If you have been touched in some way by reading this then you are already receptive to the living truth.

SEEING THE GOOD

Recently, while staying with my mother in Essex, I was very upset by all the houses that had mushroomed up in the once beautiful fields I'd loved so much in my childhood. Seeing all the bulldozers and JCBs mutilating the area, I was reminded of my recent concern about the tropical rain forests. So much of the world's beauty was fast vanishing under tarmac and being sacrificed for power and gain. Later, walking down to the beach, a dark cloud seemed to fill my mind. Even the sea could not alleviate this darkness within me; for I was reminded of the polluted waters of the world; the dying marine life, the acid rain etc. Indeed, there seemed to be no hope at all.

But then I stopped, seeing for the first time the sun dappling the water. And I realised it wasn't that there was no hope. Hope was all around me in the beauty of that spring day. It was the simple fact that there was no hope in my heart.

Suddenly, it was as if the sun had appeared from behind the clouds. I realised in an instant what a terrific responsibility we have to each other. The responsibility of maintaining a positive outlook in the face of shadow and so much adversity. To be rays of sunshine amid the cloud. And standing there in that afternoon I saw this golden example reflected all around me; in the fragrant wallflowers colouring the promenade; in the wealth of vibrant blossoms surging out from the gardens of the houses I'd passed earlier. Gardens that had been loved and cared for and where hope had not given up and left.

How often I had despaired at how little I could do as an individual to stop all the destruction taking place in the world. Yet in those timeless moments I was poignantly aware of how much I could do by just being positive. By concentrating on the beauty around me instead of the ugliness. If nature allowed herself to be dismayed by all the destruction around her, what a sad state of affairs it would be. If she gave up as readily as some of her human brethren the planet would soon die.

And yet nature never loses hope. Even on the most pitiful derelict building site wild flowers bloom. And each rubbish tip is visited by a wealth of colourful blossoms. Beauty cannot help but pour love into every empty place. Love, beauty and hope are God. And if we despair and doubt — then we doubt God.

Concentrating on the positive side of things isn't turning a blind eye to all the destruction, but rather honouring and supporting the beauty that is all around us.

And surely by positive thought we can heal and strengthen ourselves, our own environment and ultimately, the world ....

CYCLES OF BEING

If a man does not keep pace with his companions, perhaps it is because he hears a different drummer. Let him step to the music he hears, however measured or far away.

Henry David Thoreau

Living in an age where technology minimises everyday tasks to such a degree it is easy to lose contact with rhythms and cycles. If we find time on our hands we have to fill it. It's almost as if we do not dare to stop for fear of what we'll find ... or won't find. Yet if we possess the courage to stand in our time, our space without guilt or needing to justify it to the world, we can begin to experience a sense of rhythm, a harmony. This, I believe, is where God resides. Within the silence and the stillness of just being.

I was thinking along these lines when I went out to do some gardening a few days ago; removing the weeds that had spread over the borders. It had taken me over a week to dig it over, clearing a little each afternoon after work. At one time, not so long ago, I would have struggled to weed it all at once in an effort to get it done as quickly as possible. But that was before I paused to observe the rhythms and cycles not just in nature, but within myself. And anyway it's sad to think about getting something done as quickly as possible in favour of doing something else, something better. What could be better than preparing the ground ready for rebirth? The miraculous ascent of new life so symbolic of the legendary phoenix rising up from the ashes of the past to become reborn again. It's hard to believe that weeds can be viewed in a positive way. Not just as herbalists or homeopaths do when they credit every wild flower with qualities of healing and soul. But to see weeds in the light of an educational tool simply because they force us to stop, observe, attend to detail and live in the present.

I've learned a lot from these weeds with their tenacious roots which break off in the ground if I tug and pull at the growth too impatiently. They force me to smell the earth, to become involved with the soil, noticing its colour and texture. I see a whole life beneath my hand, a fragment of a snail's shell, a moving worm, and the white bulbs beneath that dream spring in the womb of winter. I have to slow down and take notice. And it takes me back, as nature so often does, to other encounters with the earth. Of the childhood gardens I made under the apple trees where grown-ups said nothing could grow. There were gardens of shells and stones. And I was sure as children are at a certain stage in their development, that the stones and shells grew. There was a garden where I planted my dreams, and although I have long forgotten these, I believe those same dreams are still growing and reproducing as I believe we meet the produce of our thoughts years later. I also had a garden where the light never entered. I called that the 'garden of shadow' and in my young mind there were fears and inadequacies that threatened to stifle my dreams.

Those childhood gardens still exist because, as ever, the outer level always reflects the inner level. Those stems of inadequacy doubt and fear still threaten to entwine and stifle my hopes and dreams sometimes if I don't keep an eye on them. I cannot suddenly decide to yank them out or else, like those tenacious weeds, the roots break off in the ground. I have to talk to them, tell them I don't want them there and coax them out individually.

Working in the garden gives me a present. It literally forces me to *be present*, to be aware. It keeps me centred, and earthed which is so vital in the fast moving culture we live in. Because when we are truly earthed we are in touch with the cycles and rhythms of life and of our own being.

It's quite simple really, we are on the earth as sons and daughters of the Creator. We are children of the earth as we have our spiritual tap root in heaven. Our substance, although having its centre in the Divine, comes from the earth and its interaction with the elements. We can't get away from it. Because if we do, we lose our centre of gravity, our balance, we become rootless and aimless.

As above, so below. Heaven above, heaven below. Again nature is a fine example of this: petals and branches above ground, roots spreading out underneath. The upper is visible to us as the below is invisible. As we too aspire towards vision and truth, there is an equal part that maintains its contact with the earth. Earth and heaven synchronised in perfect harmony.

What we do in our outer life reflects our inner process just as the seeds and embryonic growth responds to its genetic programme.

Standing still and pausing in life are vital to our well being. There is no such thing as doing nothing. But there is a quality of being, of just being. Just being is a reorientation, a listening to the inner rhythms and cycles and aligning them to the rhythm of God. But sometimes this 'standing still' and weeding can only visit us in illness and bereavement because we don't allow it admission any other time. And this is when what Thomas Hamblin would call a 'divine adjustment' can take place; when we learn to align our consciousness with the Divine.

While the world goads us on to 'achieve' and 'do' by its language of 'should' and 'must' there is an underlying rhythm which speaks another language called 'being' and 'allowing.' If we can siphon out the world's language and listen more to this inner rhythm we will find it speaks the language of the heart. And within that is a knowing that *all is well*. As we respond to this inner language the hurrying language of the world becomes less important. It even becomes nonsense, gibberish. It is important that we learn to discriminate. And even if we cannot do this, that we ask to be given the ability to discriminate.

It is so easy to become swept along by the voice of the world, which can be echoed so much in the people around us, saying we should do this, that and the other until we become deafened to the inner voice; that still small voice of God.

Back to the garden, if you don't have a garden to weed, or even to look at, don't worry. It is possible for everyone, even those partially sighted to develop their creative visualisation to make a garden. Little by little, with practice you will begin to visualise your inner garden. Maybe you will be surprised at what you see or don't see in it. But gradually you will come to love it because it is yours and it possesses its own unique quality and essence. Here we may learn a language that may not always be gleaned from books or lectures.

During the winter months when there seems nothing else to do but tend the 'grave' of the earth, it is important to draw on reserves of trust that the things we love will return to bloom again, that nothing is lost for ever. New life will emerge within the garden of nature, and within the garden of our being.

FROM BREAKDOWN TO BREAKTHROUGH

Your pain is the breaking of the shell
that encloses your understanding.

Kahlil Gibran

Breakdown is a disturbing concept whether it be a physical or mental breakdown in health or a breakdown of a community or way of life. Breakdown has negative connotations like death and destruction. In our secular culture it is a concept we are conditioned to fear and avoid. Yet we are living in an age where old systems are breaking down both on the personality level and in the world.

Living in a culture where things are defined as good or bad, black or white, it is hard to see something as part of a whole. Part of a moving changing pattern and process. Yet if the word 'breakdown' is substituted with 'breakthrough' it throws a whole new light on the picture. We accept that breakthrough is positive because it is part of a process which might have involved a long term struggle. Yet breakdown and breakthrough are part of the same process. Because when something breaks down, be it a person or a wall, it allows something else to emerge.

I find crumbling walls and ramshackle old houses reassuring in that they visually stress the fact that no physical form is permanent. Matter, however hard and durable it starts out to be, is subject to the same transformative process as nature. Breaking down and disintegration are part of a natural process which precedes new birth and development. I have been in old churches and seen crocuses flowering through the floorboards. I have walked into ruins of enormous manor houses to find a great tree growing in what was once the sitting room, and the old walls are hung with moss, fern and wild flowers.

Whether we like it or not, nature continues. Life goes on. Roads and pavements are subject to wear and tear and have to be continually repaired because nature breaks through. It cannot fail to. In time, rubbish-tips and battlefields are transformed into poppy fields. Nature is incredibly economical, making use of every opportunity to bloom and express herself. Tarmac becomes permeable. Cement crumbles. Iron rusts.

We are subject to the same laws. We cannot fail to be, because we are children of Nature. We are Nature. We grow. We die and regenerate, and this simple cyclical law is repeated many times throughout each of our lifetimes. Because we are changing, transforming as integral parts of an ancient process. Not just the process of evolution on a planetary scale, but on a personality level. We are becoming our true selves, allowing our essence to incarnate more fully into matter. And our essence is Spirit.

As our media focuses on the physical process in the world; of war, starvation, torture, the rape of the earth's resources, it is easy to become caught up in all this. Easy to dwell on the surface and shadow aspect and overlook what is happening underneath; what is slowly emerging into the light of full consciousness. But really something wonderful is happening and if we allow ourselves to become centred and drop into the still place within our being, we acknowledge this with an inner *knowing*. A deep sense of *knowing* that fills us with the belief that everything is working towards good. Everything is working out as it should be.

Because there is a planetary breakdown of resources, finances and spiritual vision, it means that something is allowed to break through. A new type of consciousness. A new awareness. Day by day, little by little we become aware of this, not just in the world, but in our personal lives. We see that through the planetary disasters humanity pools together to help, economically or through prayer. Where there is conscious knowledge of a condition there is compassion. And in compassion great healing power and love is generated.

One of the side effects of this new consciousness breaking through is that it heightens our awareness. We experience things in an intensified way. We feel not just the pain of our own body and mind, but we experience the pain of others, a sort of empathic resonance. We have compassion. Compassion means to 'feel with'.

We see and begin to understand that where there is breakdown there is the opportunity of something new breaking through where, perhaps, it would not have been able before. Instead of concentrating on the destructive death aspect we see the whole. We see the new cycle that is coming into being. And again nature is packed with analogies. I remember as a child dead heading the flowers and seeing the seeds contained inside. Think of that! Isn't it a miracle that contained within the dead flower are the seeds of the new? In dying, the flower is able to be reborn.

A friend of mine was reading a book recently and the title *Strong In The Broken Places* caught my eye. It is true. We are strong in the broken places! This truth not only applies to the physical body where a broken bone will knit together to become even stronger than before but also works out on a more universal level. Where we are strong is often where we have most been tested. What started out as weak in us becomes strong. That which is most sensitive within us is subject to breakthrough and transformation.

We are living in an age where there is a greater emphasis on healing and inner growth than ever before, not just in the world but within ourselves. Since we are all a representation of the worlds, and although it is important to acknowledge the difficulties, it is also very productive to view them in a wider context, as part of a whole. Perhaps a good analogy here is one of the tree; where the roots are contained in the dark soil, while the upper part is growing towards the light. But without the roots the tree could not be. Likewise we cannot claim our full divinity if we deny our shadow or light for that matter. The Yin and Yang symbol of two interlocking black and white fishlike figures portray this compatibility of polarities very well.

LANGUAGE OF THE MOUNTAINS

Sometimes there is no other way forward but to take one step at a time and just trust that the power which has brought us through this far will be there again. The conditions in a life situation can be so overwhelming and daunting that it just isn't possible to look or think too much ahead. All our energy and attention is needed in coping with the present. In a way, our well being and sanity is dependent on it.

I was in a situation like this once while out in Nepal. It wasn't a purely symbolic event, it was a real physical event. My life depended on it. The trekking party I was with had been caught in a blizzard in the Himalayan foothills at 14,000 feet. It was unnerving enough being marooned in a tent with just a piece of canvas between us and the raging elements outside. But the following day, and fortunately the blizzard had abated, we were forced to return to a lower camp. This was because the weather conditions were too bad to continue ascending and also another storm was expected. This meant slowly and painstakingly making our way down a 2,000 foot pass, which was narrow and icy in places. A pass with 8,000 foot drops on either side of this! Fortunately, although none of us expected this and were unprepared, we had an excellent leader who was a professional climber. But at the time, it didn't remove the fear I felt ... we all felt.

I have always suffered from vertigo and managed to keep it under control by avoiding situations that will trigger it off. And suddenly in the midst of this gruelling ascent I had an attack and I just couldn't move. All I could see was the precipitous drop and I slipped, fortunately not far, but it had destroyed any confidence I had. And then I had a panic attack where I couldn't get my breath, exacerbated greatly by the thin air at higher altitude.

Vaguely, in the midst of my fear, I was aware of a supportive arm around me and a voice saying: "It's okay we'll do this together. You take the lead with me. Just put your feet where mine have been."

It was our trek leader and slowly I surfaced from the fear and realised that I had to go on, not just for me, but for the whole group. In this situation we had to move as one. Very shaky and near to tears, I just continued taking that one step. I couldn't think of anything else. Every now and then I stopped as our trek leader paused to help someone else, if a sherpa or porter wasn't available.

And as we stopped in a safe place and I was able to admire the breathtaking views around us, my anxiety fell away. The white sculpted slopes of Annapurna South were so close that you could almost reach out and touch them. There are no words to describe the majesty and magic of the panorama before me. Mountains sculpted by time and the elements, the sun glancing against the slopes. The silence was almost deafening as if the entire world were watching with bated breath. Plumes of cloud trailed like wisps of smoke above the glittering peaks.

I was experiencing the language of these great mountains. Something I'd always wanted to experience despite my attacks of vertigo. And its language was beauty, majesty, awe. How could these wonderful qualities not be balanced by harshness and danger?

After about four hours we were safely back at the lower camp and joining the three others who hadn't been well enough to travel with us. We all felt exhausted but relieved also. And, still sitting out in the afternoon sunshine, we experienced the luxury of enjoying the views around us. Marvelling also at the steep pass we had just crossed.

I wrote in my diary: "Today I've experienced fear and

having to rely on someone else to guide me through a difficult experience. A hand is always there to aid us if we ask and make our vulnerability known. I suppose I have lived the language of the mountains. And it is as harsh as it is beautiful."

And that more or less sums it up. In the past I have never found it easy to reach out for help or make known my needs. But in order to get the help we need, whether it be on a physical, emotional, mental or spiritual level we have to recognise our vulnerability and acknowledge our powerlessness. We have to step down in order to step forward. And if we yearn to experience the beautiful and the majestic, then we must be prepared to accept its shadow side simultaneously.

My trek across the Himalayas was a wonderful breathtaking experience, and it has brought me back full circle. I know that the biggest mountains I have to climb are within me and it can be daunting until I acknowledge that I can always reach out to something greater for assistance. I don't have to make an appointment or join a queue, that help is immediate and always at hand. And sometimes, perhaps, we all need an attack of vertigo or panic to thrust us into the situation where we learn to do just that.

Another important lesson learned was just as the group couldn't move forward until everyone was able to do so, similarly as a race we cannot move forward in separation either. Although, paradoxically, growth is very often an individual experience, until that growth or awareness is utilised to help the whole, progress can never be made. We don't just grow for ourselves. We grow for the whole, for each other. It's a wonderful thought really because it gets rid of this limiting sense of isolation.

This experience, although a real situation, symbolises the mountain we all climb as individuals and as a race. Porters, sherpas, whatever guise they wear, are always there to help us with our baggage and footholds when we need them. And we always have a hotline through to the Divine, the trek leader, when we need it.

THE BEAUTY WHICH CANNOT BE POSSESSED

Beauty when it enters our lives stirs us deeply. Very often it doesn't appear if we set out to look for it. It touches our shoulder and bids us turn round and perceive it on its own terms, not ours. That beauty can manifest in a person, in an experience, an animal, flower, piece of music or painting. And as beauty touches our heart, we are filled with an overwhelming desire to own it. We see a beautiful picture and we immediately fall in love with it and want to possess it. We hear music that moves us and we want to repeat the experience. We experience the beauty in someone and we want to deepen our relationship with them. Although it is natural to want to do this, circumstances don't always make this possible. We have to accept the beauty we have experienced and let it go. Unless we can do this we are tortured by the presence of beauty, rather than transformed by it.

The captured flower withers and dies, the beautiful piece of music loses its magic, the experience we try so desperately to hold onto fades. The person who reflected the beauty that first attracted us to them changes or deserts us and we are left empty and bereft.

Beauty has always been one of my greatest teachers. She has brought me love and joy, but also pain. Not that it was her wish to bring me pain. I brought it upon myself because I tried to hold on to that which was beautiful instead of letting it go. I have always feared that if I let the beauty go, it would never return. But I have since been proved wrong. Beauty has returned to me again and again, the more I have let go. But for me this has always been a difficult lesson to learn — the letting go process. It isn't easy letting go of the things, people, events you most love and cherish not just once, but many times.

It is an act of personal sacrifice, of surrender and trust.

It is an act of nature. For just as she surrenders her blossoms and leaves to autumn each year and seems to die within the earth, so that life force which animates her returns in the spring.

Letting go of people is a very difficult and a continuing lesson in my life. It is hard letting go of relationships, to love the beauty I see in someone and give them the freedom to be. And yet freedom is the quality which I most cherish and respect both in my own personal life and objectively within the world. I have to be free, or else I feel stifled and suffocated.

Beauty whatever shape it manifests in, a priceless jewel, a dewdrop, a rare flower, is visible only in its outward form. But the essence which animates its form is invisible, ephemeral and intangible. Above all it is transitory, because beauty is a force that is fluid, that moves through matter, dips into it and leaves it. It is also eternal for its forms are myriad.

Beauty is something we all strive for, yet it cannot properly manifest within ourselves or within our own life until we let go of it first. Letting go and receptivity are the prerequisite for beauty to manifest. Beauty is Love, is Divine, is God. We are all potentially beautiful — if we let go of ourselves.

JOURNEY TO A SACRED PLACE (IONA)

I am going on a journey to a sacred place and, because you cannot be with me, I want to bring you something back. I have heard of this mystical isle for many pilgrims have travelled there to be strengthened and refreshed. Some call it the Isle of the Saints for Saint Columba once travelled to its shores. Others call it the Land of the Druids for they too moved upon its sacred shores. Still others call it the Isle of the Dove as the Holy Spirit is believed to dwell here.

It was a long journey and when I set out I was weary and tense. Inside me was a hunger and thirst that nothing could satisfy. And pain had hollowed deep into my soul.

As the train took me across fields, through cities and towns I looked at the houses and wondered if one of them was yours. Perhaps you were gazing out just then as I passed and I waved you a greeting from my heart.

Iona was at last before me and I felt its gentle welcome beneath my feet as I walked. There were many other pilgrims stepping onto its shores and the softly falling rains was like a benediction upon us, a holy baptism.

Here, where hearts were open, we gazed into each other's souls and entered the magic of true communication. As our spirits touched we knew that we were inseparable and that we were one another.

The Isle was beautiful. Every stone, each rock and grain of sand glowed as though illuminated from within. The presence of the spirit was a holy fire in the landscape. No one there could remain untouched by its reality.

As I walked I felt the strength of the rocks growing in me, gentle amethyst, dark basalt and dove grey. The white soft sands flowed through my veins and the turquoise sea pounded through my heart until I could no longer call myself a separate being.

Many of us journeyed to the Isle's sacred places and joined hands, becoming receptive to her heartbeat and offering our gratitude. On my lips was a song, a prayer for you so that you would hear it often in the deep recess of your heart.

We journeyed to the ancient sun temples where the white sands had once stretched out far beyond the sea that flowed there. Here, the rock columns became totems of power and the gentle coves resonated with the song of the spirit. Here, we dipped our hands into the crystal streams that flowed down the rocks and felt the hands of the devas and nature spirits beneath.

We climbed the hills and felt the presence of angels of Light. The wind upon our faces was the touch of their wings and the sun breaking through was the radiance of their smiles.

As I lay on a rocky prominence gazing out to the small islands washed by the water, I thought of you and tried to create this picture in my heart for you. A picture of gulls poised on air pockets, their wings the colour of the sands, of great rocks pounded by the turquoise rhythm of the sea.

You see, I wanted to bring you something precious back from this Isle. Something to hold like one of the green or red feldspar stones here, or a shell touched by the moon. I wanted to show you the tame animals here and how a cow had allowed me to place my arms around her neck as she sat there. And as I gazed into the fearless jewel of her eye I touched her spirit.

But what I have to give you is intangible as it is invisible. It is here, breathing through these words. If you close your eyes you will smell its fragrance pouring into your soul.

Dear friend, although we have never met I already feel I know you. I experience the dance of your being and know that it is my dance. And I know as you know that the hollow inside me that pain had made was really a chalice to hold this light without a name.

I DREAMED GOD WAS A TREE

I dreamed I went to heaven in search of That which shaped and set me into being.....

I found myself at the foot of a great tree. Its mighty trunk was whirled and woven with sunshine. And the star sculpted branches reaching up to forever, seemed vast enough to cradle the light years themselves.

I became small within myself and bowed beneath such a sight. Each shimmering leaf was veined with a beauty that was exquisite. The fruits were softly rounded suns which made my whole being glow with warmth and, overcome with awe, I closed my eyes. The perfumed breeze which wafted about me was resonant with silvery voices.

I knew even before I opened my eyes that the shining trees which circled the great tree were the archangels of heaven. Chanting like some majestic choir, I experienced the sound of it flowing into me, assuaging the aching hungry places within me.

I became still within myself as the chanting ebbed away. Out of this grew a mighty silence that made my heart quicken. No — it was as if the quickening were in the depths of my soul.

"Why have you come ?" the Great Tree spoke.

There was the mountain in the timbre of the voice, yet the softness of falling dew also.

The child within me replied : "I wanted to meet the One who made me."

"And ?"

"Are - you the One?"

The silence was enough; for it seemed to contain so much.

"Yes", the Great Tree spoke. "You are my fruit."

My words rushed out clumsily. "I thought — I mean —

I thought you would be remote... like cloud stuff or angel wings. But — you're solid."

"Touch me," the Great Tree invited. "Go on...."

A heat pulsed in me as the wood swelled and breathed beneath my fingers. Underneath I felt the patience of the earth and the vastness of a force which was illimitable. And the heat flowed through me in warm honeyed waves, infusing me with a sweetness that could be nothing other than pure love.

"Am I remote?" the Great Tree asked.

" No — that is impossible," I heard myself say. "You are full of light and love."

A tremor ran through the tree and the leaves quivered so that prisms of light scattered in diamonds across the soft green woodland floor.

"I am everything you are," spoke the Great Tree, "and all that you can ever be.... I am all around you. My roots run forever beneath you, and my branches uphold the deep blue of the sky."

The tree's voice was mighty, although it never once lost its healing depths. Its words seem to fall about me in gentle hues as if they contained the colours of the rainbow as well as the music of an invisible orchestra.

"... I am in your world too." the tree continued.

And I didn't know if the sadness I experienced just then was the Great Tree's or my own. "I know — but we have cut you down and turned you into money and paper we cover with untruths." I replied. " There are too few artists who can inscribe the paper which is your body with a beauty parallel with your own."

Another tremble ran through the Great Tree and through all the other trees who were the Archangels. " You cut me down and destroy me because you do not know me. But I tell you that you want me so much that you are blind to your wanting. I surrender to your chisel, your nails and steel blades and still you do not see me. And because you do not know me, you fear me."

Again the Great Tree trembled. I knew that it was not fear that caused it to tremble, but a love deeper than I could imagine which was older than the earth or time.

" When you destroy me, cut me down, burn me — this is what you do also to yourself," the tree spoke again. "For I am the air you breathe and the shade which protects you from a light and heat that is sometimes too bright to bear."

The Great Tree really was speaking in colours, for a rainbow arched out across the trees; eddying out and out to break off and become miniature pools of colour. And each colour held a fragrance which seemed to assuage a hunger that I had barely known existed in my soul.

"... I am also the food that sustains you. And the deep wisdom that rises up in a fountain to flow like honey through your soul when you, in your grief and loneliness, reach out and open yourself to me."

The tree seemed to smile and it was a dancing deep within me.

But the adult within me hung its head in shame. " I am sorry — for what we have done."

"Do not pity me." The tree spoke in deeper tones. "Pity yourselves in your unknowing.... I am eternal. I straddle the depths of time and space to birth new stars. With my breath I set the spiral and shimmering of new galaxies in motion. With my deep compassion for all that has not been created and has no voice I dance you into being. And your own world is a precious jewel that cannot be destroyed..... You can only destroy yourselves so that you return to the soundless deep which ever craves for birth."

In the silence that followed the colours had merged to

become a brightness that was pure light, and it was as if the Great Tree had become transparent so that I could see the form inside. Before me, was a most beautiful angelic being, prismatic and shimmering. But the eyes were still and somehow vast. They were the eyes of Christ, of Buddha and all the Great Masters that had ever walked the earth. And yet it was the eyes of every young child and animal I had looked at with kindness and compassion. Eyes that were both ancient and new, wise and innocent. Eyes that were the source of life. And as I gazed out across the other trees, I was able to see their proud and beautiful forms in the wood. There all around me like great tribal chieftains whose features were honed from earth and wood and leaf.

"Can't you stop us destroying ourselves?" I asked.

The tree crooned deep within itself and a hush fell upon the trees.

"No," the tree spoke at length. " But ... you can."

"I? But I am so small... There's so little I can do."

I felt the tree smiled even though its voice remained the same.

"That is because you think in terms of limitation — because you forget who you are and where you have come from... when you truly understand that you are part of creation, then you give up your isolation. By doing this you connect with me and bloom and become my fruit, then your power is limitless. You must also remember that even though the seed may feel cut off from its source, it holds everything it needs within it.... I too was a seed once... Yes, I began as you — one tiny dream in the deep mystery of being with the awareness that I had access to something far greater than myself, a source that was illimitable... I struggled for light as you have done. I felt the fear of the unknown as my buds swelled and burst open for I felt naked and exposed. But then, I experienced my first blossoming and I was infused with the incense of love and beauty.... Ah — I inhaled the quiet shining of the stars."

It was as if the Great Tree were talking in pictures, for all it had expressed flowed into my mind and every nerve and sense of my being had become attuned to what was being described, until I felt it as my own. I too experienced the lonely vigil of the stars, and yet their terrifying beauty too. I too inhaled the solidity of the great rocks and felt the patient aspiration of the mountain.

The tree sighed and a shadow fell across its trunk as if some of the light had died. "But then the blossom fell and I experienced a deep sense of loss and abandonment — as if I had fallen from Grace."

The tree's experience was my own. I had known what it was to feel a sense of union with another, only to have it slip mysteriously away, leaving me stranded in the shadows, naked but for my helplessness.

The light surged forward again, thrusting back the shadow. "But then the growth came," the mighty tree's voice was laboured. "And when it came it was slow and painful. It was growth into the unknown. I was afraid as the young bird taking its first flight into the great void. Blinded as the caterpillar in its cocoon, suffocated as the dragonfly larva at the bottom of the muddy pond, yet knowing that to give up was to die."

The vision enveloped me so that I was caught up in its shape, colour and form. I was sent spiralling out across the star systems until I finally awoke on my own planet and within the body where my spirit resided.

I dreamed that I went to heaven to see That which shaped me and found that God was a tree.

BECOMING REAL

"What is REAL?" asked the rabbit one day.
"You become. It takes a long time. That's why it doesn't often happen to people who break easily, or have sharp edges... Generally, by the time you are Real, most of your hair has been loved off, and your eyes drop out and you get loose in the joints and very shabby. But these things don't matter at all, because once you are Real you can't be ugly, except to people who don't understand."

The Velveteen Rabbit

When I consider the qualities which most endear a person to me it is their humanness, their ability to be themselves. This also applies to various teachers I have had throughout my life, whether they be academic, artistic, spiritual, Tai Chi or sports teachers. When I think of world leaders throughout history and the qualities which won them the heart and trust of their followers, it has been their sense of humanity too.

Human means divine mortal. "Hu" derives from sun and divine. How sad that we have forgotten this; that in essence, our human qualities are divine ones. In the Oxford Dictionary humanness is described as being vulnerable, fallible, kind, gentle, compassionate, sensitive and sympathetic. What richer qualities could any of us possess? In trying to hide our natural human qualities we very often evoke counter ones like jealousy, anger and fear and refer to these as human instead. Yet, we only have to admit to another person and to ourselves that we are jealous or afraid and we become human again. Denying our humanness, our divine nature, we veer towards inhumanity instead. We literally become what we don't want to be.

Humanness in another evokes a sense of realness in

others. We have all been to a lecture or seminar and as the speaker has begun we have remained separate from what is being said until the speaker has revealed a human quality, either his nervousness, his humour or simply an error, and suddenly there is a breakthrough in communication. We call it 'breaking the ice'. But it is also the point when everyone relaxes and breathes because the speaker has indirectly stated that he is human. Our heart which before might have been closed because of various expectations, judgements and criticisms literally opens. We feel an empathy with the speaker and we are ready to listen in a non-judgmental way.

It has always puzzled me why when someone dies, we credit them with superhuman qualities which we rarely acknowledge in the person when they were alive. In death, people become saints or enjoy sovereign status. It is as if death knights them in some way or perhaps, without the distraction of the body, its irritating habits and the mind's beliefs, we see people as they really are: Sons and daughters of Love, of God.

In ordinary everyday life those that do earn our admiration, and I am thinking here of spiritual leaders, are often put on a pedestal — as if they have somehow surpassed all their human habits and have a direct passage towards sainthood. Although this can be part of human nature, to project all the qualities we feel lacking in ourselves onto another, it leaves us open to disappointment and disillusion. If our 'hero', whether it be our spiritual mentor, political leader or counsellor displays a part of themselves that we are shocked that they possess, they tumble off their pedestal and we blame *them* for *our* disappointment!

Admittedly this can be partly attributed to the individual whose ego perhaps enjoys the adulation and strengthens the spell that his or her followers had put on them. After all, who doesn't enjoy admiration and praise at times? But we too are learning and growing and, within that, needing to free ourselves from enchantment and dependency on others for our unrealised dreams.

It is as if many of us have separated the spiritual from the human and filed them in different compartments. We keep our spiritual friends and activities like meditation and workshops in one file and our non spiritual human friends in another file.

I have visited friends in the past who have forewarned of a friend they wanted me to meet and added almost apologetically, " but she won't understand what we talk about. She's not into anything spiritual!" As if that makes her any less of a person. This division between spiritual and human creates a major problem in communication.

I have come to the conclusion that somewhere along the line within our journey we have lost touch with the meaning of what being spiritual and human is.

There is a tendency to put spirituality somewhere out of reach and humanness is too often accredited with weakness. In a sense we have intellectualised spirituality and made it into an abstraction. The fact is we are manifold beings, spiritual, mental, physical and emotional. There is no such entity as a wholly spiritual person any more than there is a totally physical person, but we are all human *and* divine in origin. What we see in others is what we see in ourselves, conscious or unconscious. The more our heart opens, the more real we both become. I have been with 'spiritual' people whose hearts have become closed, so great has been their need to 'do the right thing' instead of the human thing. I have been with 'earthy' human people whose openness and generosity of heart has left me speechless.

We are all familiar with Jesus words: "Ye cannot enter the kingdom of heaven unless ye become as little children."

And to me the one quality that children excel in is their basic humanness. Their realness... again and again in their natural spontaneity towards life, each other and us they bring us to our knees in their attempt to evoke our humanness. Their spirituality resides in their heart. Children know what is right and wrong. They know it with their heart and soul.

Many of us who endeavour to do the right thing judge ourselves very harshly, thereby placing impossible expectations on ourselves and others. And there is nothing further from true spirituality than judgement because it closes the heart.

When Jesus related the parable of the Prodigal Son he was illustrating the importance of humanness. The son went into the world and squandered all his wealth and drank deeply from the cup of human experience. He returned to his Father's house in rags and poverty. Yet his experiences of the world had given him enough humility to want to work as a servant in an effort to repay what he had squandered. His father instead of condemning him welcomed him back with open arms, insisting that he hold a feast celebrating his return. His brother who had stayed with his father all the time was angry at his father's leniency. His test had been to forgive and embrace his brother as his Father and accept his humanness. His judgmental heart had caused him to fail. I wonder how we would fare if we were the older brother 'doing the right thing' in the same situation?

Being human, as God made us, is accepting the dark and light within us and within others. If we cannot accept our errors and mistakes gracefully and with humour how can we accept other people's. True spirituality for most of us comes as a result of our humanness. Human experience shapes, breaks and moulds us like the potter's clay. Without it we are formless and we crack in the Master's kiln.

Being human, being real is owning our feelings whatever they are; whether they be ones of anger, bitterness, love or admiration. It is in not owning all of our feelings that we drive the ones we deny underground and they return to us distorted and evil. Evil is 'live' spelt backwards. If we deny parts of our life, they turn bad and where they could have aided us in our growth they turn against us.

If we allow ourselves to feel for ourselves then we can feel for others. The very nature of compassion means literally to 'feel with', to have empathy which is one of the most beautiful human qualities we can possess.

If our spiritual life is not opening up as we feel it should, then perhaps we need to work a little more in expressing our human qualities, our sense of heart. As we work on the personality and human level, new avenues appear within us for spirituality to manifest through. In endeavouring to 'be spiritual' rather than allowing our sense of humanity to develop, we drive what we most seek further from us.

I want to conclude here by saying that Henry Thomas Hamblin was very human too. His daughter has often shared with me how the house rang with laughter from dawn to dusk. In his home life he was very human and lived his spirituality through this essential humanness. When I think of other spiritual leaders, I think of this quality of humanness which has been so present; the Dalai Lama with his childlike qualities and ever present humour. Not to mention the man Jesus whose sense of humanity and ability to express love, sadness, despair and anger endears us so much to him.

Being real is being true to ourselves which is one of our main lessons on earth; being true to the light within our heart. Being real is becoming what we truly are — a *divine* mortal!

HOMELESSNESS

The object of life is a friendly one. Everything works together for good if we will only be friendly towards life and its experiences, and towards our fellows.

Henry Thomas Hamblin

One of our American readers and contributors wrote recently to say that the number of homeless in the States had reached a record high of 34 million, the highest ever since the Great Depression. I was shocked by the statistic. Since the measure of a healthy society is how well we look after our weak and vulnerable, it seems that for all our progress in material wealth and technology, we are impoverished in the basic human compassion and caring so vital in life.

As the compass of the year turns to winter and the days grow longer and colder I always experience a profound gratitude for a roof over my head and a place to lay my head. This has always been with me since I was a small child when to my mother's alarm I had a penchant for running up to ragged and obviously homeless individuals and dialoguing with them enthusiastically. I believed them to be the most interesting people around. Far from being afraid of them, I was attracted to their 'strangeness'. They treated me as an equal and didn't speak down to me which was 'cool'. Looking back, I can see that I was just behaving like any child with natural spontaneity and trust in the common good running through human nature.

It is easy to judge and discriminate against a vulnerable minority group. Evidence of this abounds throughout history where people have been exiled from their homes, ostracised, imprisoned even killed for anything from the colour of their skin, to their political or religious beliefs. Sadly it still goes on today in our so called modern progressive society. We discriminate against single mothers, against the unemployed or those receiving social support. We are quick to judge, but slow to understand; because if we endeavoured to understand we would totally change our perspective and drop our mind-set that these people do not deserve the same privileges as ourselves. But mind-sets keep us safe. Changing our mind-sets and adopting new beliefs is both scary and threatening.

As our thoughts turn to Christmas the whole theme of homelessness awaits our acknowledgement. After all our great spiritual master and teacher was born in a stable because there was no room at the inn. As a result of circumstances both he and his parents were temporarily homeless. And amidst our festivities and celebrations as we celebrate the millennium which is essentially the 2000th year since the birth of our spiritual world teacher, we are reminded of the circumstances around his nativity. Gazing through the lens of our relative comfort and prosperity the simplicity of this stable birth, where animals and shepherds were welcomed beside kings, must seem that we have journeyed even further away from the Christ. We complain about the commercialism, the presents, the cards which drive us further away from peace of heart and say that we have lost the magic and simplicity we had as a child. In a sense the homeless themselves are nearer to the nativity of Christ than we are with all our worldly and even religious knowledge. Blinkered by both secular and religious knowledge, that instead of offering us the security we crave imprisons us, we find our spirituality runs dry. In the words of the great master: "It is easier for a camel to pass through the eye of a needle than a rich man to enter the Kingdom of Heaven". Although 'rich man' has largely been interpreted in its literal sense of being materially wealthy, I believe this 'richness' extends to the banquet of beliefs we hold onto which segregate and divide us against each other. We have 'lost' the spontaneity, trust and natural spirituality which we all enter the world with. A spirituality that our new-born mirror back to us through their eyes which touches a deep memory within our own soul.

We judge in our ignorance, we understand or seek to understand in our wisdom.

As events manifesting within the world reflect the World Soul, or lack of it, the growing problem of homelessness needs to be evaluated and understood. The sense of rootlessness, inadequacy and isolation we experience is caused by an estrangement from our inner core. Alienation is primarily an inner condition even though it often manifests outwardly. If we feel at home with ourselves and spiritually centred, we feel at peace with the world. Our environment and how it reacts to us is a mirror of ourselves. If we change ourselves then our environment changes. That is a fact. If we change the colours in the room for instance, painting the walls yellow or white, the room will look bigger and more airy. We have transformed it.

Homelessness in the world does not go away unless the World Soul changes. Unless there is a change in our individual perspective, beliefs cannot change on a great enough scale to create a new paradigm. The homeless can be moved out of the underground and city railway stations; from the bus shelters, parks and shop doorways and put somewhere else. But the more it is denied, the more it grows. Dust doesn't stop falling because we no longer polish a room, it continues falling whether we polish it or not. We have to accept the dust as a natural condition occurring in this state of matter we find ourselves in.

But the whole situation of homelessness can be transformed, if it is understood and allowed to be integrated back into the system. The most obvious form of homelessness is the immediately visible, mainly constituted of the weaker members of our society; the drop outs who by character and circumstances have slipped through the net. These are the ones we should as a society protect, not exile. In the past these same homeless would have been imprisoned, institutionalised and drugged.

It is too easy and convenient to think that the homeless and dispossessed are that way because they have brought it on themselves or if we believe in reincarnation that is must be their 'karma'. Although in some cases this may be true, it is not always so. We only make these sweeping judgements in our ignorance. If we understood the whole picture, we would never judge. Didn't the young Gautama Buddha voluntarily give up his worldly possessions to walk the streets and become homeless ? This young man after being mocked and willing to starve to death for his truth, was to become the enlightened Buddha. Ironically, he received enlightenment after sitting under a Sal, later bodhi tree. And St Francis of Assisi one of the greatest lovers of nature, gave up his worldly wealth to serve God. World history is full of such souls that chose to become homeless in order to follow their truth and their contribution to mankind's spirituality has been phenomenal. Another prominent man donned his lawyer's suit and his former business role in the world in order to develop his spirituality in service of humanity. His name was Gandhi. So, we can't judge! We can only endeavour to understand.

Not all the homeless are alcoholics, although some of them are, as are some of us who are living quite socially respectable lives. I have met homeless people who have very strong spiritual roots and through a mixture of choice and misfortune have become exiled from their environment. In this way they have more spiritual wealth than those who work in nine-to-five jobs.

I was fortunate to meet and come to know Derek Neville, a much loved friend of Henry Thomas Hamblin. His poetry has spoken and touched many hearts that have never been moved by poetry before. He admitted that much of his honesty and wisdom had developed in the year that he had lived with the down-and-outs, selling his pen and ink copies to whoever would buy them. He wrote :

I sat on the bench,
As dirty as they were,
And as alone.
A tramp among tramps,
Looking for God
Even there,
In his rags,
In his numbed pain,
And despair.

And then I saw
The grimy hand of God
Pushing a mug of tea
Towards me along the table.

He spoke no word.
He had no need to.
I recognised him
There in the broken body,
There in the rags,
Illustrious and eternal,
My unshaven God.

I am not putting the homeless on a pedestal, merely presenting another perspective which has as much validity as the one we as a society uphold.

The most acute and pitiful sense of homelessness and

rootlessness concern those that have prostituted their spiritual roots for material roots. And here I want to again stress that nothing is wrong with materialism and money. It is part of the world of matter we live in and therefore is currently an integral part of our learning experience. But it is not the *whole* of our existence. And will not always be this way either. It is all a question of balance and getting things into their right perspective.

If material and financial considerations rule the psyche, we become slaves to the very thing that we hoped would set us free. Having money can be freeing in that it gives us access to do more things, but it can be imprisoning. Too often we become chained too our possessions. And if our self esteem and value as a human being is totally dependent on the acquisition of this money, we become disempowered by the very thing that we hoped would empower us. There is only one perennial power and that is the power we come into incarnation with. It doesn't matter whether we call it the Light, God or Cosmic consciousness. It is the unconditional love that animates the whole of life.

Arsenic and belladonna are natural poisons, yet in homeopathy used in the right potency, they are healing. Money and materialism can be medicinal if used wisely,or in the right potency. If we become too dependent on them, they can be both beguiling and highly addictive.

The seat of the real home lies in the heart. And since the heart lies at the centre of all world religions and spiritual frameworks. The heart is the lens through which we can determine what is right and wrong. The heart has a voice called conscience. If a religion or path addresses the heart then it is right. There is no indecision in the heart. The heart knows.

In our Western world where there are many distractions that may divert us from our original quest, it is important to keep in touch with what is going on in our heart. There are may beliefs that may beguile and distort our mental clarity, but if they fail to make contact with the heart, we cannot place any lasting value on them.

The major problem with this spiritual sense of homelessness is that our society as a whole upholds it. Furthermore with so much prestige attached to money, success and class status, society encourages us to become slaves to them. If our total security is placed on material structures, pension funds and insurance these foundations will always be prone to disintegration and breakdown. And because we have exiled ourselves from our roots; creativity, light and love, what we have cut ourselves from becomes like an angry sea, beating relentlessly against the friable walls of security. The sea will always be there. Walls fall down. Time dissolves barriers, but the unexpressed and untamed remains and becomes more formidable. As the psychologist C.G Jung says: 'What we resist, persists.'

Although we may not feel we can do much to help the homeless other than by making donations, our individual work on an inner level can have a far reaching effect. This work is acknowledging and affirming our spiritual home which is within. By closing the door to the outer world and seeking stillness within, if only for a few minutes throughout the days we align ourselves with a consciousness greater than our own and which is sometimes referred to as Cosmic Consciousness. In aligning ourselves with our inner home and affirming our own true spiritual nature, we meet the true spiritual nature in all people which in turn 'awakens' the memory of this spiritual home within others on a deep level. As we become part of this re-homing process within ourselves and others we help transform the collective consciousness, affecting and energising the cells into a higher state of being — which is essentially navigating   the World Soul homewards; from spiritual impoverishment to spiritual abundance.   Honouring and acknowledging the true spiritual nature within another is the greatest gift we can ever give to anyone.

CAN WE SPEAK FOR THE ANIMALS?

I am not spiritually minded because I am a vegetarian, but I am a vegetarian because I strive to be spiritually minded. As one advances in spiritual understanding, flesh eating becomes repugnant and one is happier without it — at least, that has been my experience.

Henry Thomas Hamblin

I have often received a number of enquiries from readers concerning Hamblin's thoughts on animals and the cruelty which so often befalls them. Despite Hamblin's incredible wealth of wisdom and spiritual knowledge, he rarely preached at people concerning what they should and shouldn't do. He suggested, listened, spoke freely where he thought it was appropriate and trusted to the growing spiritual awareness in each person to lead them forward on their journey. He respected all religions, all faiths and although intrinsically following the Christian teachings, had friends and associates from all spiritual backgrounds, and faiths.

Hamblin's great concern for cruelty to animals in the name of vivisection, sport, fur trade exports and plain greed only came over in the Monthly Notices in the 1930s where he appealed to readers often to be aware of our fellow creatures and petitioned on behalf of donkeys and ponies being used down the coal mines.

As the collective consciousness undergoes transformation through all the escalating changes taking place in the world and within our personal lives, our ears become more sensitised to our conscience which many perceive as the God within us, or the 'still small voice'.

In general people are not so much concerned with global issues such as pollution, deforestation,war, human torture and animal cruelty as to what *they* can do personally to make the world a better place. The inner conscience of humanity is growing at such a rate that many of us want to take responsibility rather than the old familiar way of foisting the blame on someone else and sitting in judgement. It is far too easy to blame others and opt out. This old way of thinking was a self-absorbed way of protecting our own principles, denying the spiritual truth, and consequently disempowering ourselves. It was a way of making us feel better in the midst of insoluble problems. But this doesn't work any more because using well worn scenarios of blame and denial does not make us feel better. Quite the contrary. Instead of empowering our sense of moral rightness, it has belittled us, made us feel uncomfortable and resentful of new ways of thinking that challenge our own.

So what do we do with this huge slice of blame which can be an umbrella for a seething cauldron of emotion beneath? Do we blame ourselves, chastise ourselves ? No, because that too is the old way of thinking. Instead, we learn to forgive ourselves and, if need be, ask forgiveness of what we have injured, working from the premise that we probably did the best we could at the time. We resolve to begin again with renewed determination and insight. Simultaneously, we must be aware of the gaping traps awaiting us of criticising others around us for not holding the same beliefs — when we only left their way of thinking five minutes ago! And also not straining at the leash trying to convert everyone which can give way to a form of mental arrogance? Neither must we allow ourselves to become caught up in judgement, blame and accusation again. Others have their own path to follow, their own conflicts to resolve. This is not so much a tall order for us to swallow as a *willingness* to change our thinking and so change our behaviour and life. It is only our thinking that holds us prisoner, not the issues themselves which come in the form of tests we are asked

119

to face and learn from.

And *always* inside every problem lies the opportunity, the key that frees us. Our own struggling and inner conflicts will give us the opportunity to develop compassion and humility, qualities which are nearer to the heart of God than all the piety in the world!

I am fortunate in that from being a small child I found the idea of eating dead flesh pretty repulsive. At home, I asked if I could sit in the garden to eat my lunch. There, out of vision behind the garage, I would toss my meat over the neighbour's fence!

At boarding school where I had three meals a day, seven days a week and it was hard to hide my eating habits, I was often teased about my vegetarianism. In my teens, I was challenged continuously by older people around me who themselves felt challenged by me. So, I certainly didn't do it because it was going to make my life easier. Today, it is so much more acceptable to be vegetarian, and supermarkets go out of their way to cater for this changing dietary consciousness so that now it's considered 'cool' by many of today's young vegetarians. Meat is no longer part of the 'macho' image.

I wasn't a saint either, I drank and smoked like most other young people and was rebellious in a quiet way. Hopefully, I am not a fanatic either as I have been in situations over the years where someone has invited me to lunch, and my request has been forgotten or not passed on, and I have had meat put in front of me, I have eaten it so as not to offend the person who has gone to so much trouble and goodwill to feed me — and thanked the animal! Again this exemplifies our need to be mindful and that if we rigorously apply the same well worn formula to every situation, we quickly become rigid and inflexible.

Today it is commonly accepted that all life is interconnected. What we do or don't do affects the overall pattern. How we live our life, relate or don't relate to each other has an effect.

And here I have to say that doing nothing is just as powerful as acting. Action and inaction are what we apply to every situation in life. It is through choosing between these two great poles of being that we make and shape our journey, we leave our trail, our hallmark of self. We are talking about karma here. Action involves commitment and the responsibility it brings. Inaction too involves responsibility. Used appropriately action and inaction are very powerful mediums of manifestation and change. Used wrongly, they can hurt, maim, kill and affect thousands of lives.

Sometimes it is appropriate to do nothing when perhaps it means joining a political party and going on a march which we know could cause violence.

Sometimes the very effect of doing nothing and allowing something which we know is wrong to take place around us, is one of the greatest sins we can ever commit. Conscience will tell us so. What we give out returns to us in some form or other. What we don't do, returns to us too. Speaking out for what we believe to be true *does* take courage but we must remember that we 'depend not on our own strength'. We are given strength to do what we know and feel is right. Difficulty overcomes us when we depend only on ourselves.

When our action or inaction can affect the quality of life of another living creature, then it is important we do what is right, follow that voice of conscience. We may lack courage — but true courage comes from the *heart*. The heart does not doubt, the mind does.

For those of us who are concerned about our fellow creatures who rarely have a voice in this material world, we *can* have an effect. It is not my intention to make anyone feel guilty if they are not vegetarian, but rather understand how what we do and do not do affects life around us. Making choices based on 'shoulds' gives rise to resentment and ill will which does neither ourselves or the world around us any good.

Be prepared to change.

The whole world is changing as life is ever striving to perfect itself. Old beliefs are giving way to new emerging ones. We have to learn to move through the conflicts instead of being bogged down by them. When I was at primary school over thirty years ago it was commonly believed that milk, high in calcium, was good for children. It was mandatory to drink a carton of milk daily, whether we liked it or not. Today this is no longer the case as discoveries have found that milk can be harmful to us, causing a lot of allergies and in many cases being indigestible to humans. Milk also boosts the huge calf industry, forcing cattle to bear calf after calf under often intolerable conditions.

What choices do we have? Because we always have a choice and with choice comes power. If we cannot do without milk maybe we can choose to have organic milk where cows roam free in the fields, or soya milk. "Ah" — someone might say, "aren't soya beans genetically engineered—isn't that harmful?" It depends whether we are genuinely concerned about our health or are using it as excuse. Our conscience will tell us.

I don't wish to go into the atrocities of animal husbandry so well highlighted by BSE swamping our media, but to look at how what we do affects the whole; where we put our power - what we give our power to.

Another strong argument is, shouldn't we put humans first? Aren't humans more important? Yes, we're so important that if we don't change our thinking and behaviour we are heading towards not only making much of life extinct, but ourselves too. And the only hope we have is to consider the 'whole' of life — life in relationship with ourselves. This begins with our attitudes to the young, the defenceless, to animals and nature. We are dependant on life, the planet — the planet and nature are not dependent on us. We are caretakers of the planet, not rulers.

Hamblin writes on the World day for animals (October 4th) which is dedicated to St Francis: "The universal observance of the world day for animals can only be secured by every leader of public opinion becoming the Voice of the voiceless. In addition, of course, we must be practical and do what we can to avoid inflicting suffering on animals by anything that we do. For instance, we can refrain from killing animals and birds for our food, using furs for our clothing, and we can also refuse to use vaccines and cosmetics which are the product of vivisection being used upon us."

Since this was written in 1940 there are numerous medicinal and cosmetic products that are listed as alternatives to many of the mass produced ones and who claim they do not use animals. Today there are alternatives to Hormone Replacement Therapy (HRT) which inflict such cruelty on mares. Additionally, if you cannot find an alternative do not punish yourself, just do what you can.

In most respects, we have the *choice*, the *power* and the *conscience* to at the most totally transform our lifestyle in harmony with God. At the least we can be mindful of how we are living our lives.

ALIGNING WITH PURPOSE

Unless I feel I am in touch with a sense of purpose, I find it very hard to access sufficient energy and motivation to get through my day; however good my intentions. Even if I have sufficient strong will to master the tasks set before me, without a sense of purpose something vital is missing. Heart is missing.

Purpose can mean different things to different people at defining points in their life. Purpose can be the family or a partner so that even if a challenging work situation presents itself each day, the family and partner can evoke sufficient motivation to keep on keeping on until the situation changes, or we change it. Some careers give more sense of purpose than others; caring and vocational professions are generally invested with a strong sense of purpose, whereas other careers may be more of a means to an end, increased prestige and financial security. Similarly, even the most menial job can be purposeful where the money may be utilised to finance another more creative lifestyle or a work that expresses our inner values.

Where purpose is invested solely in career, status, finances and even family, purpose can easily be knocked sideways by anything that jeopardises our position like loss of a job, or death. Yet becoming increasingly more common today is a loss of purpose in young and successful people who have achieved all the things they had wanted; family, prestige, money. They have literally lived out their purpose but at the same time in the midst of their career experienced a state of spiritual impoverishment. Where this used to be a point reached in the mid 50s (like Hamblin who left his successful business life in his 50s because of a sense of spiritual impoverishment), it is being reached at an increasingly earlier age.

I personally know of at least a half dozen people in their

early 30s who have reached the peak of their careers as lawyers, managers and business executives who have left their high powered jobs to look for a career that aligns them with their true sense of purpose, rather than the purpose dictated by worldly values. Many of them have taken a drop in salary and position in exchange for a work that holds greater meaning for them. This only goes to prove that spirituality is not a commodity to be developed in one's later years, but a quality to be held and nurtured all through the life. Neither is it something to be edited in and out of the life at various points of the week or times of the day. Spirituality surrounds and imbues us, if we allow it. Neither is it a quality to be utilised in converting the 'ignorant majority'. We are all spiritual beings and therefore all treading an intrinsically spiritual path in varying state of awareness. Once comparisons are made between other people and other sects, criticism, exclusiveness and spiritual arrogance sets in. Spirituality comes from the heart, not through the intellect or emotionalism, therefore it is accessible to us *all* at *every* point of life. As Hamblin wrote: "We are spiritual beings living in a spiritual universe..."

So far we have looked at purpose on a personality level; one invested in the values of the world. We refer to this often as 'my purpose'.

But what about a higher sense of purpose that is more 'Thine' than 'mine'; a purpose which can waken us to the purpose of humanity on a global level. How do we define our purpose other than through the vehicle of the personality?

Up until now, many of us have loosely defined ourselves as having a higher or spiritual purpose with a somewhat abstract commitment to 'allow ourselves to be divinely guided' or to 'follow where the spirit takes us.' On one level we are handing over our life and responsibility to the Divine, God or a Higher power, but on another level we are

125

negating responsibility for this purpose. Consequently, we wonder why we lack any clear direction or way of manifesting our higher values into being. In a sense, we are going unconscious to our purpose.

I believe that we have reached a point in our spiritual level where we are being invited to take a step further and consciously align ourselves with our purpose and move from the abstract to the concrete by bringing it into form. Then we can allow ourselves to be 'guided' and 'led' by the Divine, but first we need to take responsibility for this ourselves.

The obvious question now would be to ask; " How do I know what my purpose is ?" And " How do I know if it comes from some higher order of being or just from my personality, my desires".

One of my tutors in Psychosynthesis once described this difference very succinctly: "The Self* *invites*. The personality *demands.*"

And as many of us know there is a profound difference between invitation and demand. Invitation involves an opening of being and surrender, whereas the whole issue of making demands involves being driven, being pushed, bullied and beaten into a level of submission which we all know about when we are being hard on ourselves.

So... taking the invitation... we will find that our purpose can be revealed through our values. What are our values? What do we regard as precious in our lives? Another way of defining our purpose is to reflect on what makes our heart sing.

What makes your heart sing? Think back...What made your heart sing as a child? What makes your heart sing now? What makes you feel fully alive?

This may not be a vocation as such; it might be walking in nature; taking our dog for a walk; being with our children, our grandchildren; singing; writing, taking photographs, swimming, yoga etc.

You will find as your values begin to emerge, your heart will open and your breathing alters; other images may flow in that are interconnected.

It may be from reflecting on this that your purpose is one of being more fully yourself; opening up to ideas, inspiration; beauty; creativity; healing; peace; love and so on.

Once you feel yourself aligning with your purpose you will experience a sense of rightness. The next stage is to look at how you bring your purpose into form; how you make concrete the abstract. How do you bring this quality into your life? Perhaps you have always been aligned to your purpose and not known it. If you don't already manifest it into form, are there ways in which you can do this? If your purpose is to live your life more fully, are there ways you can allow this into your life? Is there something you have always wanted to do but have been afraid to do? Take a risk, take a step.

Aligning with purpose which is essentially transpersonal*, is opening to one of the qualities of the universe. Bringing it into form is a way of manifesting it through the vehicle of the personality into the world and making it physical. If we do not make a conscious effort to commit to our purpose, we cannot fully live our lives; because we are creatures of purpose and meaning. And we are here to bring our purpose into form; to manifest it in the world.

This sense of purpose and commitment once acknowledged will see us through lean and barren times when we are confronted with loss, disappointment and illness. By realigning with our purpose we access a consciousness and light that will shine through our work and life.

Once we have committed to this higher sense of purpose we will experience an opening of the heart and quite probably

Beyond the personality   127

have some sort of spiritual experience that will confirm and acknowledge our direction. This is often experienced as some sort of 'honeymoon experience' where we feel protected and strengthened. But then, inevitably, comes the difficult times when the shadows come to test our light. This testing may not even be tangible, but rather a battling within ourselves. We may be overwhelmed by feelings of unworthiness. We may feel afraid to be visible in our purpose; where we may evoke reactions of envy and judgement as well as admiration from others. It is easier to step back, retreat and put ourselves down, this is called the repression of the sublime; where we as well as others around us downgrade our purpose, often on an unconscious level.

Until recently I didn't realise I was guilty of repressing the sublime in me, of betraying my purpose; because in many ways I have ample opportunity to express it in my writing. Yet, my writing is only one facet of my expression and without having to come into form beyond my words, it is relatively unchallenging. But in making myself more visible by bringing myself into form, no longer hiding behind my writing, I am challenged on a deeper level of my being to be true to myself.

Being true and aligning to higher purpose is literally living our life more fully, allowing our inner light to shine. It is very different from being hooked into various ego defences where we may feel we need to convert or control the other.

Again this simple barometer of being can tell us where we are: the Self *invites*, the personality *demands*.

But as the personality reflects and aligns to higher purpose then it automatically becomes strengthened and less pulled by the desire nature.

PURPOSE AND PASSION

Each one of us is born at the right time, in the right environment, and we can be truly successful only when we do our right work and follow our true path.

Henry Thomas Hamblin

Following on from *Aligning to our Purpose*, I have been thinking how difficult it is to actually move to the final stage, of not only living our purpose, but bringing it into form, into matter. Spirit is always seeking channels and opportunities to manifest in form, reflected so much in nature and our own natural process of incarnating into the world. Too often though, ideas although aligned to purpose, stay in the head and never come into form. It is easy to talk very eloquently about ideas and even become moralistic in saying that we would do such and such if we were a particular person, politician, or doctor, but much harder to *walk* our *talk*. Business meetings abound globally where ideas are proposed, but never followed through in order to bring the embryonic form into manifestation. Why is this then? Why is it so difficult to bring purpose into form, providing it is the right purpose, not one based on greed and gain by abusing the impoverished and vulnerable.

I believe that it is not because we are inherently lazy and afraid to do the work; rather that we are inherently afraid to act. In a world that demands guaranteed success, it is hard to walk our talk if it goes against these fear — based values. Our purpose diminishes in the face of risk; we want the money before we act; we want some sort of guarantee that it will work which is tantamount to demanding from a meteorologist a hundred percent accuracy. As the fears of the world impinge on our inner values and take hold, we gradually become disempowered and our energy diminishes. To compensate for feelings of inadequacy and failure we justify ourselves saying that it is better to keep on the highway of the known rather than follow the slip roads that could lead us to a breakthrough beyond our wildest dreams.

The only qualities that can save us are a passion and commitment that will give us the courage we need. But again passion and commitment need to be the right kind, based on higher values rather than personal ones. We don't need to be reminded of how passion driven rulers have committed themselves to personal grandiose ideals at the expense of thousands of lives and enforced poverty.

There is nothing wrong with passion and commitment as long as it is aligned to higher purpose and values. The sort of passion I am talking about is the one that has driven women and men throughout history to make massive breakthroughs in their areas of work, like Marie Curie and her discovery of radium which involved grave risk and ultimately her own death. Rachel Carson, also a scientist who wrote *Silent Spring* while battling with cancer and the barrage of insults by male scientists who saw her as a threat to the scientific fraternity. Then there was Martin Luther King and his fight against racial discrimination. Gandhi and his struggle for peace, both of whom were killed for their beliefs, yet because of their passion and commitment, initiated vast changes in public thinking.

Focusing more on present day values there is the work of Wangari Maathi, once one of Kenya's leading scientists who gave up a glittering career in academia in exchange for fighting environmental reform. Despite enormous opposition, including being beaten up and receiving death threats, she has spent 20 years averting desertification in Kenya by planting trees. Then there is the amazing but true story of the girl, Julia Butterfly Hill's struggle to save the Redwoods. This slip of a girl spent two years up a 1000 year old redwood in California and did not come down for two years. She lived 180 feet in the air, on a four by seven wooden platform protected by a piece of tarpaulin. She stayed there even when her feet turned black with the cold and she came close to dying, blasted by icy winds blowing at ninety miles an hour. Even when loggers tried to fell trees in her direction, shone light up into her eyes so that she couldn't sleep for days and her food supply stopped she stuck it out. She said: "If I walked away from this destruction I'd be just as responsible as Pacific Maxxim". She prayed for strength, hour by hour and once when she wailed out that she couldn't take any more, she describes how she entered into deep communion with the redwood. She could feel it telling her: "We've been here for thousands of years. We've lived through everything, so can you." And so she described how she forgot her self pity.

As the situation settled, she spent her time in the tree talking to politicians, radio stations on cell phone and last Christmas she came down. A deal had gone through with the timber company. Against all opposition, she had saved her redwood and three acres of land around it. Furthermore, her behaviour has become an inspiration to many.

When Einstein said; "Progress is made by unreasonable people", he didn't mean those on the main highway who sacrifice their soul purpose to greed and power, but those who travel the slip roads to unveil the Kingdom of Heaven within.

It is within us all to be able to act this way. But the fear doesn't go away and the guarantees don't come until we commit ourselves to our ideal. When we act 'as if', doors open, supply comes, strength pours in — but not before.

I am reminded of the ramshackle old offices we came to when we arrived here. Leaky, tumble-down sheds that were below freezing in winter and soared into their nineties in the summer. I couldn't get the idea of new offices out of my head;

the conditions were so appalling that neither myself or any new staff could continue to work there. It was either new offices or I would go. Those of you who remember at the time will remember how we began with £500 and gradually through your belief in us, the money came trickling in. Then Hanne Jahr, my assistant editor at the time, started appealing to charities for grants and gradually within two years it happened.

But if we had waited for the offices to materialise, the money to come in without acting first, it would never have happened.

I am reminded here of Anita Roddick, the amazing entrepreneur, who founded The Body Shop. She began in a back room, like Laura Ashley, recycling her bottles, making her products by hand. She began with no financial backing, but she began. And with her commitment to the environment and working for the Greater Good she and her colleagues have become one of the leading businesses today. Now she is even contacted by prestigious organisations like Harvard and Stanford on her business expertise. She writes; "It is all too easy in business to be distracted by profits, the technology, the cost-effectiveness, the delivery systems. What is important is never to lose touch with what lies at its heart and soul — to remember why you are doing it in the first place." She also writes about the loneliness of having a new vision, a dream; that, because it is different, not everyone shares it until the hard work is achieved and they can see tangible results. In fact bringing something into form that has a new vision is not always welcomed, it can be an isolating experience.

We have talked about realising and living our dream through the lens of historical and contemporary figures. But what about you?

One of the most common comments I have met with from people who visit is; "It's all right for you. You have a special gift. You were born with that spirituality."

And I always say in polite terms that that's a load of rubbish! I want to say that sometimes I sit in my office to write, and I have no idea what to write. I just trust that the right thing will come. I sit in a state of expectancy, trusting and believing that something will emerge. Sometimes it can be very frustrating indeed.

It was frustrating this time because I had it in mind that I would write something on the ego and our misunderstanding of its value in our life. I had written something on this for another magazine, and thought I had saved a copy so that I could use some of my ideas here. It is quite rare for me not to write anything from scratch but I have had a lot of work on recently and been pushed for time. Yesterday I went through my disks, looked in my computer and realised I hadn't made a copy on the hard drive. The only thing I could do was write to the publisher for a copy of it but that would take too long as I am in the midst of two deadlines. This morning I had to accept that this wasn't what the 'Universe' intended me to write. I drew an angel card for this morning and it was 'surrender' and that's what I have had to do.

This is a clear example of aligning to purpose and being ready to surrender all that we think is important or right to higher values. It isn't easy, and I don't know whether it gets easier, but it is the only way.

Aligning with our purpose which builds the commitment and passion necessary for action and change in the world, is the only way we can become part of the solution, rather than the problem.

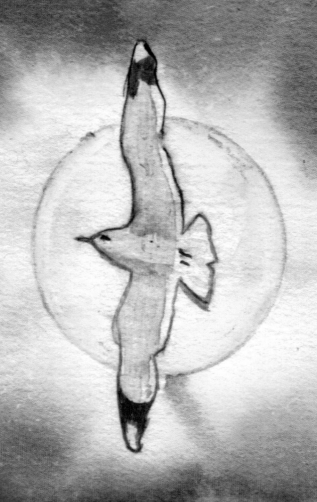

PART FIVE:
GOING BEYOND THOUGHT

GOING BEYOND THOUGHT

Head knowledge is a hindrance; that is why in order really to know God we have to lay aside all that we have learned about God ... We have to go beyond thought in order to enter into the ultimate truth.

Henry Thomas Hamblin

"I have all this knowledge, I've been to all these lectures, I've read all these books," the young man exclaimed, spreading his hands in exasperation, "and I'm still no nearer to solving my problems. What do I do with this knowledge?"

I met this young man at a counselling group several years ago and his genuine frustration lingers in my memory. His outcry spoke to everyone in the room. It was something we either had all experienced or were in the midst of experiencing.

It was an obstacle which Henry Thomas Hamblin encountered within his own spiritual journey as he writes: "It is one thing to know with the head, and quite another to know with the heart." His words echo the truth which so many mystics and other serious aspirants have also found. The problem is that quite often, although we have all the knowledge, it has failed to penetrate our being. Mental knowledge is rather like the glamorous icing on the cake. It merely sits on it because it is too hard and rigid to penetrate the cake. When knowledge through experience is worked into the heart something rather wonderful happens. It becomes changed into wisdom which, because it is malleable, is like the honey which penetrates the cake. Wisdom permeates our whole being.

Mental knowledge too often sits in our head.

Knowledge, however, has a very positive use. It is a valuable tool for education and, research. Without it, we would be creatures of instinct. Through expanding our degree of understanding, it can provide us with much insight into situations in need of change and improvement. But always, it needs to be tempered with wisdom. Time and time again mystics refer to the higher mind and how it can only be found through the heart. True, the mind can give us wonderful mental alacrity in being able to talk **about** religion say. We can play mental gymnastics with various theories and concepts without actually touching into truth. It's rather like learning geography at school. Learning about different cultures and nations without actually having visited them. Many people like myself have only found countries to come alive when we have visited them.

Because of all the learning facilities available to us at present, it is tempting to believe that if we amass enough information, go to enough lectures, read enough books we will have a deeper understanding. And this may be true to a degree, but what we are really looking for is a sense of peace. And the mind alone cannot give us that sense of peace, we have to access the higher mind for that.

We only have to look at ourselves and the people around us all stuck in our belief systems, each feeling we are right because we have grasped a small facet of the truth, to see the evidence of this. We cling to facts and ideas in order to maintain a dwindling sense of security, rarely realising that it is this mental rigidity that causes us to feel insecure and isolated from our Greater Consciousness. The unknown and untried become a quagmire of fears and doubts, instead of the spontaneous adventure the universe intended it to be. In contrast young children have a playful spontaneity and trust which makes them almost fearless in their sense of adventure. And yet many of us will agree it is this fearlessness and trust which precipitates a heavenly state of being. And this is what I believe Christ meant when he said, "Unless you become as children, you cannot enter the state of heaven". Because children have a strong sense of heart they do not get caught up with the icing on the cake. How many times are we bowled over when a young child will innocently come out with a statement that goes beyond intelligence? A statement that holds a wisdom that we have invariably long lost touch with.

"I do not know Truth through the intellect; I know God who is love through love ... I cannot know him through my mind, but only through my heart," writes Hamblin.

I find this statement both interesting and reassuring coming from a formerly successful businessman who had explored almost every mental exercise in the 'book' in order to secure inner peace and truth. And yet as many before us have discovered for themselves, we cannot travel far spiritually with the mind alone. Like the young man at the beginning of the article, we reach that mental impasse which gives rise to spiritual aridity. We encounter the brick wall that a lot of Tibetan lamas use as a symbol of the outer mind to meditate before.

It is the wandering in the mental wilderness, where everything we have learned and believed to be true is stripped away, that we may make our first encounter with the Divine, that Greater Love. I know in Christian mysticism there is a period of deep loss and inner poverty, and indeed Hamblin himself referred to this time as the 'stripping' period. Within this stage of inner poverty, where all the mental beliefs and clutter that we have accumulated about God no longer serve us, our hearts open. Our need is great enough to invoke a plea of desperation to the Master, the God within. Into our broken and empty hearts flows that peace, wisdom and understanding that the world with all its desires cannot give.

It's quite justifiable to ask ourselves here, why acquire any knowledge if we've got to let go of it? What's the point?

But then again we have to access 'higher mind' and gain a clearer picture rather than become caught up in the treadmill of mental activity which can make us even more rigid. No one can teach us the futility of the intellect in accessing the Greater Truth; it is something we can only discover through our own personal experience. True wisdom is the higher mind working in conjunction with the heart.

THE FREEDOM OF TRUTH

"Re-examine all that you have been told.
Dismiss what insults your soul."
Walt Whitman

We all live within a network of beliefs about ourselves and the world, consisting of religious, scientific and moral doctrines which we hold to be true. These maintain our outlook and perspective of the world; making sense out of seeming chaos and allowing us to live more comfortably in a world that is often full of paradoxes and disharmony. Our beliefs give us a measure of harmony and inner peace. Or at least they *should* do.

But whatever beliefs we have about ourselves or the world these are subject to change, whether we like it or not. And this is where we can confront obstacles and difficulties. Because we are continually evolving both collectively and individually, it is a natural process to shed whatever is no longer needed; let go of whatever has outlived its usefulness. It is at this point of greater growth and development that we may start to question our beliefs. This, although uncomfortable, is healthy and perfectly natural. It is a natural breaking down of waste products before anything new can emerge.

Yet, sometimes out of fear and inability to accept what is happening, we hang on even tighter to our beliefs. This makes whatever is within us, struggling to emerge, much more difficult. Growth is a continual surrender and letting go; a series of mini deaths and mini births. If we dig our heels in and resist the impulses for the new, then our beliefs imprison us rather than free us. They no longer serve us. And because our inner state is so often reflected in the immediate environment around us, the people and the groups we attended even the books we once enjoyed no longer bring us any solace. Rather it seems as though everyone and everything is working against us, when really it is we who are working against our Greater Self. If we are not aware of what is happening we can pull our beliefs even tighter around us until they become imprisoning. We may condemn everything outside us as wrong, so consequently the world has become a very unfriendly place - all because of our rigid belief system.

"The truth shall set you free," the Christian teaching states clearly. It is often in the light of this gentle reminder that we are able to ascertain whether our beliefs are working for us. Are they freeing us from the prison of self ? or have they got a grip round us like a boa constrictor?

If we hang onto what is disintegrating and dying, then it is quite natural that it will work more as a poison than a medicine.

So what do we do when this breakdown in belief happens? Do we go searching for another teacher, another belief system, another religion and begin all over again? This may work out in many respects when our beliefs have expanded to such a degree that the old framework has broken and we need a new one. But since our beliefs are often going to undergo some sort of transmutation which will affect a transformation in our self, we cannot change our religion every time. If our religion is based on truth then it is unchanging. But too often truth is distorted to suit our ego and personal will and like a garment that isn't looked after, it becomes out of shape.

Perhaps instead we need to look at what is struggling to emerge within us and forcing its way through the core of our belief system. The Christian teaching tells us that the Kingdom of Heaven is within. In fact the perennial wisdom, spiritual and religious, ancient and new echo the same message; that what we seek is within us. Basically, the Truth we seek is within us. And it is the truth which is wanting to emerge into our everyday consciousness. If however, our beliefs have confined us, making us rigid in our ideas this emerging truth demands that we break free of our imprisoning bonds. We have outgrown our cage. Our beliefs need to be broken down in order to accommodate the Greater Truth. So if we can live with the discomfort a little longer and not grasp onto our old dying habits, we can entertain the perspective that we are actually expanding to our full potential. This expansion becomes, instead, an exciting adventure rather than a threat to our well being.

Truth is very simple, and this is what makes Hamblin so popular; his simplicity of style and practice. It is all the embellishments to truth, the beliefs we hang onto which make it so complicated. Beliefs are really the excess baggage we carry around with us, which we think give us more comfort, but in fact can become a burden. It is beliefs that cause us to judge and criticise each other and the world. If we took away all the beliefs there would only be truth left, no more judgement.

Quite naturally, this has emerged from my own inner process of letting go of some of the beliefs that I have had about the world and myself. I have been in what is classically known as a state of purgation, of spiritual cleansing. Because this process of allowing all my beliefs up to the surface for renewal has been a cyclical process in my life, I have come to understand it. Without the stability of my beliefs I can feel very naked and vulnerable. I can feel out of my depth and a sense of worthlessness. Furthermore it isn't something my *personality* self invited, rather my *soul* evoked it for my greater growth.

In a world of change, conflict and growth it is reassuring that the foundation we set our tent upon is unchanging. The knowledge that truth embraces all is a universal understanding. Truth works by uniting, rather than separating. Because Truth is God, it underlies all great world religions. The beliefs may be variable, the wrapping different, but the truth of service, love and forgiveness are the same.

Today the market place is full of beliefs; ones that may range from being vaguely different to our own, to being the exact opposite. All these beliefs say that they are right and the others are wrong. And in this approach there is something missing, the element of truth, because truth is all embracing.

This diversity is reflected too in the average supermarket, where there may be up to six variations of baked beans, tins of tomato and where the cereal counter is a whole city in itself! We might go for our usual trusty brand or try another one for a change, or perhaps like me stand in complete bewilderment by what is before us! Yet however many variations there are of a single product, most of the time they are fairly much the same. Baked beans are baked beans, regardless of their package and there is only a finite amount of things you can do with a tomato!

It is the product that is important, not all the embellishment. The product is the truth, the reality, not the label or beliefs that are attached to it. It is too easy to lose sight of the original product in our modern obsession with labelling and advertising.

The truth is unchanging. God is unchanging. Love is unchanging. And in a world of constant change this is reassuring.

If our beliefs that we are carting around us no longer serve us then we only have to throw them away. It isn't the beliefs that are important but the truth. And the truth is that you and I are sons and daughters of God, each one of us manifesting a unique aspect of the Divine. We are all seeking truth, whatever name we attach to it. If I condemn you, then I condemn myself. If I judge you, then I judge myself. We judge only in ignorance, never in wisdom. If I embrace you, whatever your outer form, language, colour of you skin, then I embrace myself.

SPOTTING THE SIMILARITIES

*The exterior part of a religion does not matter much —
although it is about this that people quarrel so bitterly — it is
its inner meaning and experiences that are important. The end
and object of religion is Divine Union, and if another soul
attains to this blissful state by a different road from that which
is the only one that can be used by us, let us be glad and praise
God, instead of wasting our time explaining to him that he is
wrong and our way the only one. Let us all be broad minded.
Our Lord said, when speaking from the superconsciousness,
wherein He realised that He was consciously indwelling the
advanced souls in every nation and religion: "Other sheep I
have which are not of this fold."*

*Let us be glad that this is so, and rejoice in that the Truth
can be found in many different ways.*

Henry Thomas Hamblin

One of the puzzles I particularly enjoyed as a child were
the'Spot the Difference' cartoons. Here, by studying two
seemingly identical pictures side by side you ringed the details
on one picture that were different to the original.

But in retrospect, I can see how the underlying principle
of the game is the basis for a greater part of our everyday
reality. It is much easier for us to 'home in' on the differences
between people or cultures we feel wary of, rather than find the
similarities, the relatedness between 'us' and 'them'. From an
early age we learn to section and divide the differences between
people, religions, political parties and judge them accordingly
as good or bad, negative or positive.

Generally, children are very good at spotting the
differences, not because they have been encouraged to think
this way, but rather because they are genuinely curious. If you

listen to young children, their judgements are neither good or bad. In fact impartial observation is used rather than judgement. And in this there is a genuine interest and acceptance. The innocence with which these observations tumble out can be a source of embarrassment or amusement. "Why is that woman black?" Why does that man limp?" Why is that person wearing glasses?"

Each explanation given will be systematically filed away for reference and just accepted. The differences, from this perspective, are based on uniqueness which is a part of life rather than prejudice. Preferences based on personal experience may come as a result of these peculiarities or arise from normal personality differences. But preference as we shall see is very different to prejudice.

We all like to feel that we are not prejudiced, that we are in fact open minded and accepting. And if we do feel strongly about certain values, then we consider ourselves well justified and 'in the right'. After all, prejudice has negative connotations and we like to believe that in endeavouring to live the spiritual life we are moving on from this limiting perspective. Yet, most of us whether we care to admit it or not, are guilty of being prejudiced in some way and need some reminding of this as well as guidance.

So, let's look at prejudice and see what it actually is. The dictionary definition cites that it is a lack of tolerance, a discrimination towards a sect of people either because of religion or culture. It is a tendency to pre-judge situations or someone before we have experienced them.

We can see immediately that this way of thinking is not only in direct conflict with the Christian teaching of love, tolerance and forgiveness, but all major world religions. Prejudice is acting against divine Love. It isolates and imprisons us within a straitjacket of our own making. Any way of thinking that limits the expression of the heart and soul, estranges us from God. Instead of becoming open and spontaneous, we become inward and controlling.

At the beginning of each New Year we are invited to make new resolutions that will carry us into a more holistic future. Since we cannot make any long lasting resolutions until we embrace a change of attitude within ourselves, it is important to look at this issue of prejudice, not just in the world but within our own life. It is my belief that it is our personal prejudices that prevent us moving forward to meet new experiences in openness and love. To the extent we hold prejudice in our heart towards a fellow human being or authority, we limit ourselves. Acceptance, tolerance and openness are fundamental prerequisites for living the spiritual life. Since the small child has these qualities, it is not something that has to be learned in an intellectual or academic way, rather it is an attitude, a way of thinking that we need to unlearn.

Just because another person's belief system, whether it be a political, or religious one, is different to ours it should not merit our contempt, but rather earn our respect, or in the case where it is harmful to life, our compassion. Contempt is based on prejudice which is due to a fundamental lack of knowledge and ignorance based not so much on an inability to understand, but an inability to even want to understand.

We know that strong belief systems and values are based on fear rather than love and acceptance. There is an underlying lack of trust of the self and God. Trust cannot be built up if there is an unwillingness to change. Give trust the freedom and space to grow, then like a small seed it will slowly burgeon.

We have to understand that it is our fear of change that prevents us reaching out to embrace others and their belief systems. We feel that in accepting others, we would have to change our own beliefs. And if we can accept that prejudice is based on this deep-seated fear both within ourselves and others we can already change our thinking by being more tolerant and having compassion. We know how crippling fear can be, how dehumanising and demoralising. We all know how it can render the noblest of us powerless. Understanding how and why prejudice manifests helps us to be more tolerant of ourselves and others. Condemning prejudice is **not** the answer, but understanding **is.** It becomes infinitely easier to embrace that person or culture's fear in love, rather than the prejudice and hatred itself; for in reaching out in this way we heal ourselves. We cannot help doing this because it is divine law. "Whatsoever you do unto others, you do unto me..."

As change is vital to our growth and continued evolution, it should be welcomed rather than fought. I have to speak from my own experience when I say that often, often when I have reached out to the things that I feared it has been these that have given me the greatest joy, a new lease of life even. I have actually come to love the things that I feared. Those old dragons really do become the greatest of companions — if we allow them too.

So far we have been concentrating mainly on prejudice and differences and we have seen how this can distort our sense of reality and build walls between 'us' and 'them'. If we can accept that nearly everyone in the world wants to be loved, accepted and feel part of a greater sense of community we can use this as our basic building block for world relatedness and unity. What sets out as a way of changed thinking, ultimately becomes a way of being too. That is why it is so important to begin with ourselves. As there is a new group of world scientists emerging like Rupert Sheldrake, Fritjof Capra etc (the late David Bohm) who maintain that everything in life is interconnected, we too have a very important part to play in this time of world change and transition. Using the spider's web as a model, we can see that the movement of a single thread affects the whole. There is no separation, only in our inability to see this. Each individual thread comprises an integral part of the whole web. What we do and think about others has a complementary effect, not only from a karmic viewpoint, but due to the genuine inter-connectedness of all life.

We can go a step further in talking about the levels of life; such as the physical, mental, emotional and spiritual ones. In order to function as a human being to our full potential we need to feel connected on all these levels with ourselves and with others. In this age of computers, those of us who work with them are able to perceive on an everyday practical level how all the programmes are interconnected. Basically a program is a pre-written formula that allows the user (you or me) to perform certain tasks like word processing or accounting. Today these are commonly called 'windows' which can be taken literally. These windows provide insight into different working levels, yet all of the windows are connected to the Program Manager which, if you like, is the presiding body over all the other work functions. For example in the offices here, we might want to update your subscriptions, so that is going into one application, and yet at the same time, we might want to write a letter to you or design a letterhead by opening another 'window'. As many as three or four windows may be running beside the 'active' one. And understandably it is common in the early stages to get out of one's depth and feel caught up in a labyrinth of boxes and messages, but always if we go back to the Program Manager we know where we are. To me the Program Manager is the centre, and all the others are expressions of being. Relating this to ourselves, we can see that we are all functioning and working through different 'windows', but underneath we are linked to the Program Manager, the divine Centre, the Creator.

As William James writes so eloquently, "We are like islands in the sea — separate on the surface, but connected in the deep."

LOVE IS THE KEY

It was a great day for me when the realisation came to me that love is behind all life's experiences. And that the secret of life is simply love. Directly, I realised this I could see that love had been at work in my affairs all the way through, and that the disorders of my life were due to my working against love instead of co-operating with it.

Henry Thomas Hamblin

If I am able to distil two phrases from Hamblin's writing that have affected me the most then I would choose his: 'Love is the key to every situation in life.' And: 'Trust the current that knows the way.' These two simple truths are both practical and spot on. In fact, they are almost too simple.

Then why is it so hard to apply them in our daily life? Like all truth, they have that essentially ageless, yet childlike quality to them, appealing more to the heart and intuition rather than the intellect. Since most of us who have had to struggle with the fear, doubts and anxieties of the lower mind will know, the mind is the slayer of the real and the beautiful. Even when we have grasped the validity of a piece of wisdom and integrated it into our consciousness, the lower mind will start to question it and tricks us into believing that our judgement is wrong. That is why we so often regret not having listened to our intuition. Things quickly go wrong and become confused the moment we allow the lower mind to become our master.

Like Christ stilling the waves, we have to pacify the feverish outer mind before it makes us its slave; for that is when our life stops being our own and we feel like a leaf in the storm, at the mercy of the elements.

But neither can we make our mind our enemy and try to deny it expression; for like an angry petulant child, it will rebel against the restrictions that we impose upon it. Will alone is not enough; for the lower mind is a trickster, seizing every opportunity to fool us and win us over until we collapse in exhausted defeat. Once we pursue the spiritual pathway, the mind becomes more cunning and rather than fighting against us, it will even appear to be working with us. Since the development of the spiritual muscles threatens the validity of the lower mind, it will be on its best behaviour, applying a different tactic altogether. It may kid us into believing that we are very spiritually evolved so that our egos are so stoked up with this illusion we want to believe it ourselves. After all, the future of the lower mind is invested in our belief in this image of ourselves!

Here, it is helpful to apply humour and a little insight to our spiritual growth. And we all know there are countless opportunities in life to help us not to take ourselves too seriously! Incidentally, humour and humility very often go together. The insight comes from knowing that this unwieldy lower mind which seems to be in direct conflict with our unfolding spirituality is really there for our greater inner growth. It tests our mettle. It is not there to belittle us, but rather help us become the shining jewels we are by exposing us to chisel, flame and heartache.

Do we not so often learn through our children? Through their testing us again and again to the very core of our being we become more capable of love. The more heartache our children inflict us with, the more we seek to understand, forgive and love. The mind although a petulant child, seemingly working for ever against us, is our teacher too.

The mind will always be with us on our journey through life. That is an irrefutable fact. Additionally, the mind has a purpose just as everything in our life has purpose. And if we think we can overcome it with our will or by resentment, we have to think again.

There is only one way we can overcome the mind and that is with love. Yet, love does not so much as overcome as transform. It is the pure magic that works miracles within ourselves and throughout our life.

If we can work *with* our mind rather than fighting it, then trust and love, which were mentioned at the beginning of this article, become a lot closer to a way of being rather than something impossible to attain. We can perhaps say: "Okay, this is my mind up to its antics again, but this isn't the whole of me. I am not just my mind. I am more than this." This allows us to detach from our mind a little and gain a more objective perspective. The mind will immediately become calmer, little by little, because it is not being threatened or denied, rather we are accepting it as a part of us. Every living thing wants to be accepted, and the mind is no exception.

Usually, when I meditate and I think this applies to most people, my mind will always dream up innumerable things I need to do until I am full of restlessness. But I have a tremendous advantage here. I have been through this scenario many times before. In fact, it is perfectly normal. It is the same if you had a dog and someone comes to the door; the dog will bark and bark. But eventually it will grow tired of barking when the visitor goes away or settles inside the house. All things pass. This is a fact.

So we can say to ourselves: "All right, mind. I know you are there." In acknowledging it, the mind loosens its grip. It relaxes...

We also know that as we sit there, listening to soft music, slowing down our breathing, relaxing our body or applying whatever technique we use, we experience a sense of peace; a coming home to harbour in a safe place that has always been. We have entered our 'still centre' and touched into a peace, however brief, that is infinite and eternal, a peace that underlies all creation. A peace that is God. It is as if we really have sunk into those 'everlasting arms beneath' and we experience a great love. However briefly we experience this peace, we never forget it. It has somehow inscribed itself across our hungry soul. In fact it is this peace, this love, that draws us back again and again to seek it. We are willing to go through the outer discomfort, the grumbling lower mind for that sense of peace. There is something very special about this peace because it is not a worldly one. And the love we feel places no expectations upon us. It is non-judgemental and unconditional.

And so this is where we return to love again; this unconditional love which so many of us feel we do not possess because we easily become confused with need and desire. Unconditional love is pure love, the distillation of the Divine. It just gives of itself for the sake of love. And to a greater or lesser degree we have all experienced it, either through the love of a child, pet, flower, tree or through some creative project or something we simply love to do. Although we may not be aware of it all the time, it is always present. And if anyone were to ask us how this unconditional love came about, we wouldn't have any answers; because it is not something that has been developed. It has always been there.

To the extent we experience this unconditional love is the extent to which we truly live. Contrary to some beliefs, unconditional love can be passionate, although love can be gentle and peaceful it can rise to great heights to protect or express what it loves, and there is nothing wrong with this. Passion is a part of nature, art and God.

This is the type of love that has the key to open all doors. And it is a key we all possess, although we may hide it or even feel ashamed of it because it is not something the outer world understands . . . But *we are* the outer world. What exists in the outer world is the outcome of what is taking place internally. Always we stand in front of a door between the outer and inner world with the key on our side. And love is the key.

What we need to understand is that unconditional love is when God loves *through* us. We become channels for this to be. It is not something we have to work at, fight for, overcome, tear at, it simply 'happens' when we surrender, let go and really trust the current that knows the way.

NEW VISION

Founded in 1921 by the late Henry Thomas Hamblin, a practical English mystic, and presently edited by Stephanie Sorréll, this bi-monthly, charitable magazine is devoted to the spiritual life and applied right thinking.

The underlying theme of NEW VISION is based on a greater understanding of our spiritual centre of identity, and instructive, helpful guidelines are given to enable us to apply this greater understanding to our everyday life. The steadfast practise of this teaching can transform our life and has done so in countless individuals for over 70 years.

The magazine is not an attempt to establish a new cult or religion, but rather a sincere effort to help people of all shades of religious belief, or none), on their transformative, spiritual journey. It meets a real need in the hearts and minds of many who are seeking for a deeper meaning to life and inner stability. Its precepts can be read and practised by anyone. The emphasis is not so much on belief but rather on personal spiritual experience, as the articles and poems by its contributors indicate.

NEW VISION has a large circulation and goes to a multitude of people in many walks of life all over the world, many of whom find it provides a "life line" through difficult and troubled times. It is published at a price that is much less than the cost of production and distribution, so as to bring it within reach of all. It is subsidised, however, by the kindness and loyal support of readers who are in a position to give more than the minimum subscription asked.

Titles by Henry Thomas Hamblin

The Message of a Flower	ISBN 1-903074-03-7
The Little Book of Right Thinking	ISBN 1-903074-00-2
My Search for Truth	ISBN 0-9531597-7-9
The Story of my Life	ISBN 0-9531597-8-7
Within you is the Power	ISBN 0-9531197-2-8
The Power of Thought	ISBN 1-903074-02-9
Life Without Strain	ISBN 0-9531597-9-5
Divine Adjustment	ISBN 0-9531597-6-0
The Open Door	ISBN 0-9531597-3-6
Life of the Spirit	ISBN 0-9531597-4-4
His Wisdom Guiding	ISBN 1-903074-01-0
The Hamblin Book of Daily Readings	ISBN 0-9531597-5-2

Also Recommended:

The River That Knows The Way
Edited by Stephanie Sorréll
ISBN 0-9531597-0-1

The Inner Temple by Hanne Jahr
ISBN 0-9531597-1-X

New Vision — a bi-monthly magazine
(formerly *Science of Thought Review*)
founded by Henry Thomas Hamblin

for further information contact the publisher:
Science of Thought Press Ltd.
Bosham House, Bosham, Chichester,
West Sussex PO18 8PJ, England

Telephone/Fax: +44 (0)1243 572109
Email: scienceofthought@mistral.co.uk